Struik Pocket Guide
for Southern Africa

Insects

Eric Holm

Department of Entomology
and Zoology
University of Pretoria

ILLUSTRATED BY
Elbie de Meillon
and others

STRUIK

Contents

How to use this book 3
How to recognize insects 4
Relatives of insects 5
Key to the orders of adult insects 6
Silverfish or fishmoths 9
Cockroaches 9
Mayflies, dragonflies, damselflies 10
Earwigs 11
Termites 12
Praying mantids 13
Crickets 14
Locusts and grasshoppers 15
Stick insects 17
Lice 17
Bugs 17
Antlions, mantidflies, lacewings 24
Beetles 25
Flies and mosquitoes 36
Butterflies and moths 39
Wasps, bees and ants 44
Some inconspicuous insects 49
Life cycles 51
Collecting and breeding insects 53
How to preserve your insect collection 57
Glossary 61
Further reading 62
Index 62

Struik Publishers (Pty) Ltd (a member of the Struik Publishing Group (Pty) Ltd)
Cornelis Struik House
80 McKenzie Street
Cape Town 8001

Reg. No.: 54/00965/07

First published in hardcover 1986
Second impression 1988
First published in softcover 1993
Second softcover edition 1995

Copyright © text: E. Holm 1986, 1995
Copyright © published edition: Struik Publishers 1986, 1995
Copyright © illustrations: E. de Meillon 1986, 1995, except for the following:
E. Holm. (Page numbers in brackets are followed by figure numbers as placed from left to right, top to bottom, on each page.) (6); (9) 5; (10) 4, 5; (11) 2-7, 9; (13) 2; (14) 3, 4, 7; (15) 2-5; (16) 2, 3; (17) 1, 2, 5; (19) 2, 5, 6; (20) 1, 6; (21) 1, 3; (23) 2; (24) 2; (25) 5; (26) 2, 4, 5; (27) 4-7; (28) 1, 2; (29) 2, 3; (30) 1, 2; (32) 5; (34) 1; (35) 2, 5, 6; (39) 4; (41) 2, 3, 5; (45) 4; (46) 2, 3, 4; (47) 2; (48) 4; (49) 1, 2; (50) 1, 2; (51); (52) 1-3.
The following illustrations were reproduced with permission of the Department of Entomology, University of Pretoria, from Insects of Southern Africa, Butterworths, Durban, 1985. (Scholtz, C.H. and Holm, E., eds.)
J.D. Agnew (10) 2. G. Arnold (title page); (4) 1; (44) 3. K. Bidlingmaier (32) 3. J. Boomker (29) 5. A.L. Capener (22) 2. W.G.H. Coaton (12) line drawings. J.F. de Villiers (23) 4-7. W.L. Distant (9) 4; (21) 2; (22) 3, 5; (41) 4; (42) 3; (43) 7. H.J.R. Dürr (33) 3. E. Grobbelaar (4) 2; (14) 5; (20) 3, 4, 5; (24) 4; (34) 4; (38) 3; (42) 1, 2; (45) 2; (47) 4; (50) 3-6. S.F. Henning (39) 1; (42) 6; (43) 8; (44) 1. G. Jacobs (37) 4. M. Johnson (28) 5, 6; (35) 1, 4. A.J. Prins (48) 3. G.L. Prinsloo (44) 4. S. Schwartz (24) 6; (25) 3; (42) 5; (43) 6; (44) 2; (49) 4. B.R. Stuckenberg (36) 1; (50) 7. N.J. van Rensburg (31) 4-7; (52) 4-8. L. Walles (15) 6; (17) 6; (18) 2, 3; (45) 1. A. von Peez (32) 2.

Set by McManus Bros (Pty) Ltd, Cape Town
Reproduction by Hirt & Carter Ltd, Cape Town
Printing and binding by CTP Book Printers, PO Box 6060, Parow East 7501

All rights reserved. No part of this publication may by reproduced, stored in a retrieval system or transmitted, in any form or by any means, electronic, mechanical, photocopying, recording or otherwise, without the prior written permission of the copyright owners.

ISBN 1 86825 831 9

How to use this book

This book is intended for use in the outdoors, whether you are hiking, fishing, mountaineering or simply spending a day in your garden. The illustrations and text in this book will promote a greater awareness and understanding of the smaller 'game', the insects that share our world.

As there are some 100 000 species of insects in southern Africa, the book cannot hope to show representatives of all groups. The examples described, therefore, are species from the most commonly seen groups, and of these only the most representative or common species have been illustrated. The descriptions and illustrations make it possible to recognize other members of the group, especially if the key to the orders (page 6) is also consulted.

Our insects are classified into 27 orders, with certain orders being divided into two or more suborders. Some orders have few species and are described in a single paragraph, while others, such as the beetles which comprise about two-thirds of all insect species, warrant proportionately more space. In these large orders, the various species are grouped and discussed as part of the family to which they belong.

The terminology has been kept simple, and is explained in the next chapter and the glossary. Both common and scientific names have been used and, for those who want a more serious involvement with entomology, there is more information in the chapters at the end of the book and a reading list has been included. Afrikaans names have been included at the end of each main entry.

Insects have life cycles during which their size and appearance may change drastically (see page 51). The illustrations mainly show adult specimens, and sizes given are those for the adults of the species. Unless otherwise stated, the measurements are taken from the tip of the head to the end of the abdomen, excluding any appendages. For most groups, illustrations of some of the immature stages are included. These stages are usually difficult to identify and therefore are treated in less detail.

The most important function of this book, however, is to help reveal the fantastic world of small miracles of insects.

How to recognize insects
Anatomy

Adult insects have three main body parts: the head, thorax and abdomen. On the head there are usually two large compound eyes and often two or three small simple eyes on the forehead. The head also bears the two antennae and the mouthparts, of which the mandibles are usually the largest. Mouthparts vary according to diet – some are used for chewing, others for sucking or licking.

The thorax has two or four wings in the flying species, and always six jointed legs. These consist of a hip or coxa, a femur, tibia and foot or tarsus. The abdomen may have tails or cerci and/or an egg-laying tube or ovipositor. The cerci may be formed into claspers (see Earwigs, page 11), and the ovipositor may be transformed into a sting, as in bees and wasps.

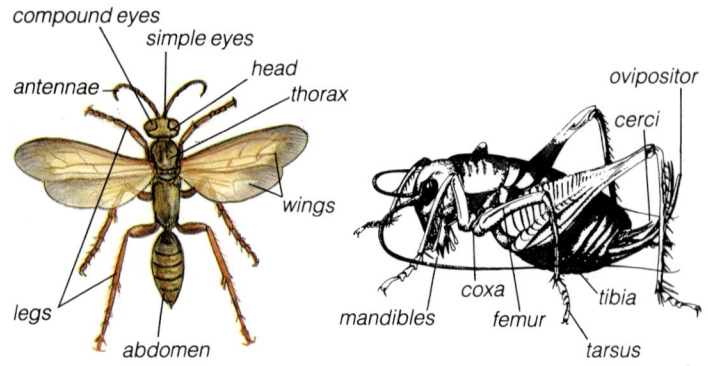

Insects are classified into orders and families according to differences in their anatomies. It is therefore important to note the differences in mouthparts, legs, wings and abdominal appendages. In the Key (pages 6-8) and throughout the text, the details which characterize the various groups are given. It may be necessary to use a hand lens to see some of these details, particularly in the smaller species. Colour and general shape are very unreliable features to use when identifying insects, since many species of completely different orders may resemble or even mimic each other in these respects.

Relatives of insects

Before we can start identifying the various orders and families of insects, we should of course know which animals are insects and which are not. Insects belong to the large group (or phylum) *Arthropoda*, which are animals without an internal skeleton but with a tough skin composed of movable segments. These include crabs, crayfish, centipedes, millipedes, scorpions, spiders, ticks, mites and a few lesser-known groups. Of all these, insects are the only winged animals (although not all insects can fly). They are also different in that they have six legs, and three well-defined divisions of the body, namely head, thorax and abdomen. It is for these reasons that the following relatives of insects are *not* insects:

Scorpions. The thicker the tail relative to the pincers, the more poisonous the scorpion. Very long-lived, nocturnal, often carrying their offspring on their backs. Live in burrows, under rocks or bark. Exclusively predators. Head and thorax not separated, eight legs.

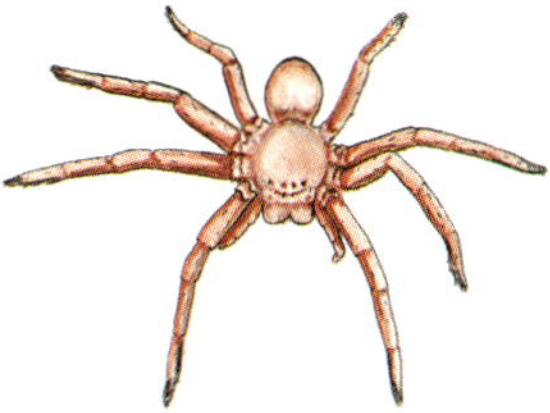

Spiders. Several thousand species are known to occur in southern Africa. Size 1-150 mm. All are predators: some use webs while others are hunters or ambushers. Head and thorax not separated, eight legs. Only three are dangerously poisonous: the violin spider, the black widow (or button spider) and the *Sicarius* species.

Centipedes. Relatively few species, flat, multi-segmented, one pair of legs per segment. Nocturnal predators of snails and insects. Size up to 150 mm. Often brightly coloured. Claws on head can inflict painful sting. Live in humid environments.

Millipedes. Long, cylindrical and multi-segmented, with two pairs of legs per segment. Can curl into a tight spiral. Scavengers and plant eaters. They produce irritating secretions and poisonous gases, and are left alone by most predators. Up to 300 mm in length. Black, brown or with yellow bands.

Ticks and mites. Eight legs, no discernible thorax, sac-like abdomen, mouthparts adapted for sucking. Ticks are notorious blood-sucking parasites of animals, and also carry diseases. Mites are usually very small, often scarcely visible. They live on plants, as parasites on insects, scorpions or other animals, or as predators of small arthropods.

Key to the orders of adult insects

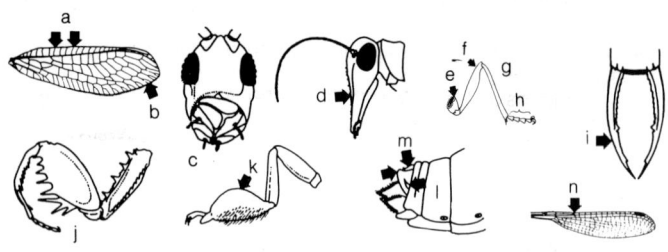

1. Three many-jointed 'tails' on tip of abdomen, always wingless
   Fishmoths (THYSANURA) .... p. 9
   – Two 'tails', or none. If three 'tails', they always have wings .... 2.

2. With two or three 'tails' and wings, 'tails' longer than body
   Mayflies (EPHEMEROPTERA) .... p. 10
   – 'Tails' absent or shorter than body, winged or wingless .... 3.

3. With four transparent wings, each with notch in front margin (fig. **n**)
   Dragonflies, Damselflies (ODONATA) .... p. 10
   – With or without wings, never with notch on front margin of wings .... 4.

4. Laterally flattened, bird and mammal parasites, coxae at least as long as femora (figs. **e, f**)
   Fleas (SIPHONAPTERA) .... p. 50
   – Not with combination of above characteristics .... 5.

5. Two cerci (fig. **l**) on sides of last abdominal segment, sometimes formed into pincers. Last abdominal segment divided (fig. **m**). Mouthparts always for biting, abdomen not separated from thorax by a deep constriction .... 6.
   – Cerci absent. Last abdominal segment undivided. Mouthparts variable, abdomen variable .... 17.

6. Tarsi (fig. **h**) with one to four joints .... 13.
   – Tarsi with five joints .... 7.

7. Fore- and hind wings either similar in size and shape, or hind wings transformed into long thin ribbons .... 8.
   – Wingless, or hind wings much broader than forewings, folded below forewings at rest .... 11.

8. Head elongated and beak-like, with mandibles at tip (fig. **d**)
   Hanging flies (MECOPTERA) .... p. 50
   – Head not elongated .... 9.

9. Wings densely covered with hair
   some **Caddisflies** (TRICHOPTERA) .... p. 50
   – Wings with little or no hair .... **10.**

10. Wing veins branched near wing margin (fig. **b**), fore- and hind wings similar or hind wings ribbon-like
    some **Antlions** and **lacewings** (NEUROPTERA) .... p. 24
    – Wing veins not branched near margin
    some **Alderflies** (MEGALOPTERA) .... p. 49

11. Back-plate of first thorax-segment shorter than those of other two thorax-segments
    Stick insects (PHASMATODEA) .... p. 17
    – Back-plate of first thorax-segment longer than others........................ **12.**

12. Front legs grabbing (fig. **j**)
    Praying mantids (MANTODEA) .... p. 13
    – Front legs normal walking legs
    Cockroaches (BLATTODEA) .... p. 9

13. First joint of tarsi inflated (fig. **k**)
    Web-spinners (EMBIIDINA)... p. 49
    – First joint of tarsi normal.. **14.**

14. Cerci formed into hard pincers without joints (fig. **i**)
    Earwigs (DERMAPTERA) .... p. 11
    – Cerci not hardened and pincer-like... **15.**

15. Antennae with segments rounded, like a string of beads. Social insects.
    Termites (ISOPTERA)... p. 12
    – Antennae different. Social or solitary insects... **16.**

16. Wings all similarly thin and transparent
    Stoneflies (PLECOPTERA) .... p. 49
    – Wingless, or with forewings leathery and thicker than hind wings
    Crickets and **locusts** (ORTHOPTERA) p.14

17. Head with mouthparts on two sides dissimilar, skewed (fig. **c**). Tarsi with no claws, but a small sac on the end
    Thrips (THYSANOPTERA) .... p. 50
    – Mouthparts and head symmetrical. Tarsi normal, with one or two claws (fig. **h**) .... **18.**

18. Forewings hard shells, covering thin hind wings when folded, and meeting in a straight line down the middle of the back. Biting mouthparts
    Beetles (COLEOPTERA) .... p. 25
    – Forewings only partly hardened, or thin throughout. If the abdomen is covered by a hard shield, this shield shows no middle line. Sucking mouthparts .... **19.**

19. Tarsi (fig. **h**) with one to three joints, thorax and abdomen never separated by a deep constriction.. **20.**
— Tarsi with five (rarely four) joints. If only three joints occur, then thorax and abdomen are separated by a deep constriction .... **22.**

20. Mouthparts piercing and sucking, like drinking-straws, and held in a rostrum (modified, grooved lower lip). (In scale insects all appendages, including mouthparts, are reduced and barely discernible.)
 Bugs (HEMIPTERA).. p. 17
— Biting mouthparts (if sucking, they are hidden inside the head and there is no rostrum).. **21.**

21. Antennae several times as long as head
 Booklice (PSOCOPTERA).. p. 49
— Antennae at most as long as head
 Lice (PHTHIRAPTERA) .... p. 17

22. Wings covered in scales, sucking mouthparts which are mostly very long and coiled below head
 Butterflies and **moths** (LEPIDOPTERA) .... p. 39
— Wings smooth, or with little hair or only a few scales. Mouthparts never coiled below head .... **23.**

23. Wings covered in hair
 some **Caddisflies** (TRICHOPTERA) .... p. 50
— Wings without hair or having at most hairy fringes. Sometimes wingless
 .... **24.**

24. Wings with many cross-veins between first two long veins (fig. **a**) .... **25.**
— Wings with no or only one cross-vein between first two long veins....... **26.**

25. Wing veins branched near wing margin (fig. **b**), fore- and hind wings similar or hind wings ribbon-like
 some **Antlions** and **lacewings** (NEUROPTERA) .... p. 24
— Wing veins not branched near margin. Hind wings much broader than forewings.
 some **Alderflies** (MEGALOPTERA) .... p. 49

26. Biting mouthparts (mandibles) present, four thin wings or wingless
 Wasps, bees, ants (HYMENOPTERA) .... p. 44
— Sucking or licking mouthparts (no biting mandibles), two thin forewings (with hind wings reduced to small clubs), or wingless
 Flies and **Mosquitoes** (DIPTERA) .... p. 36

Silverfish or fishmoths
(order Thysanura)

Very agile, wingless insects that live off cellulose and starch, and are usually found in dry plant litter or under rocks. Some species live with ants or termites, others inhabit human dwellings where they damage paper and starched materials. Characteristically have three long 'tails' and a body covered in scales. About 60 species, 1-15 mm.
☐ **Silwervisse; vismotte**.

winged roach scavenging

Cockroaches
(order Blattodea)

Flattened, fast-running scavengers and omnivores, some species are household pests but most are free-living. Nymphs are similar to adults but are wingless. Most species are winged, and have leathery forewings that fold flat on the body over thin hind wings.

Some species never develop wings. This may apply to the females only, or to both sexes. Wingless females sometimes carry offspring on their bodies for a while.

Characteristics of cockroaches are backward-inclined mouthparts **(a)**, large flat pronotum (backplate) covering the head **(b)** and long coxae (hip-joints) **(c)**.

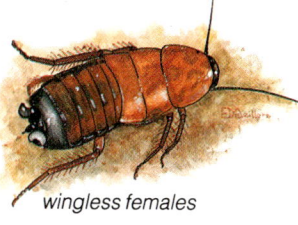

wingless females

In many species the female carries an egg-pouch protruding from her abdomen until the eggs hatch **(d)**. At this stage some simply drop the pouch, whereas others re-absorb the pouch and feed the hatched young inside their bodies. About 200 species, 5-50 mm. ☐ **Kakkerlakke**.

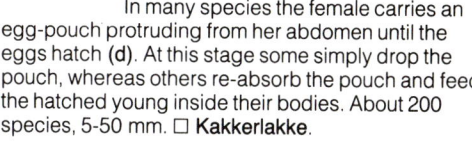

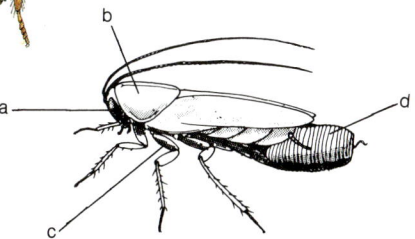

Mayflies (order Ephemeroptera)

Always found near water. Adult is very short-lived – often only one day. It emerges as a dull dun then moults to become a clear-winged specimen, with two or three 'tails', large forewings and small hind wings. The adult does not feed. The nymph lives on the bottom of streams and pools, has three (rarely two) 'tails' **(a)**, and gills **(b)** on sides of abdomen. Feeds on detritus and plant material. About 200 species, 4-20 mm.
☐ **Eendagvlieë**.

Damselflies
(order Odonata: suborder Zygoptera)

Often seen sitting on grass or reeds near water, with wings folded backwards over body. Wings about equal length, transparent, with thin bases and a notch in the front margin. Eyes widely spaced. Hind body long and thin. Feeds on insects, which it catches in flight. Slender, predacious nymph lives in water, and has leaflike gills on tip of abdomen. About 80 species, 35-85 mm wingspan. ☐ **Waterjuffers**.

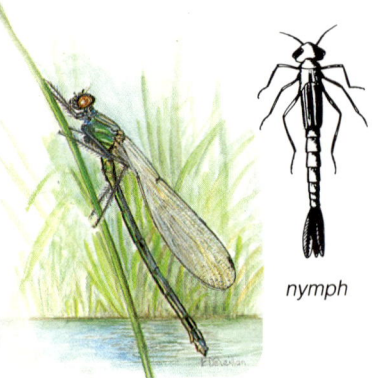

nymph

Dragonflies (order Odonata: suborder Anisoptera)

Resemble damselflies, but have large eyes that meet on top of the head, broader hind wings, and wings are usually held sideways when at rest. Dragonflies are territorial. The male sits on a perch and attacks any other dragonfly that enters his territory. Females fly through territories and eventually mate with a male. Dragonfly males are more beautifully coloured than females, but only acquire these colours some time after emerging from the nymphal stage.

Mating is complicated: the male deposits sperm in a pocket behind his thorax (breast-part) (**a**), then grabs the female behind the neck with special claspers (**b**). The female then collects sperm from his pocket (**c**). They often fly in this tandem position while the female lays her eggs in the water.

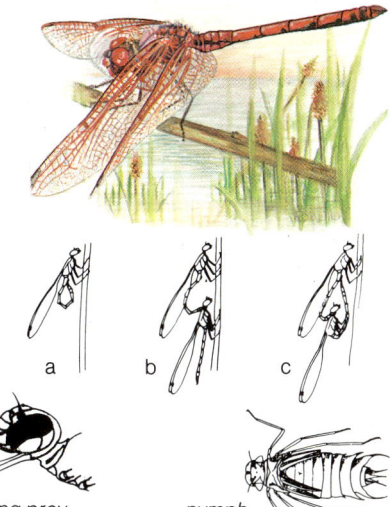

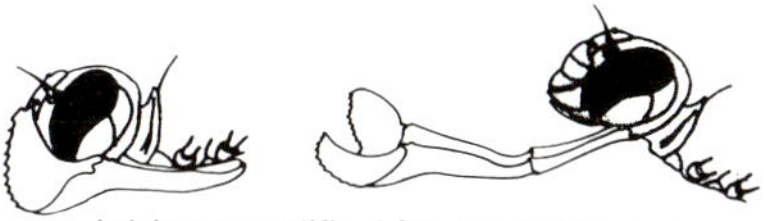

labium modified for grasping prey   *nymph*

Nymphs of dragonflies and damselflies are aquatic predators, catching water-insects, tadpoles and even fish. The labium (lower 'lip') is uniquely modified into a telescopic clasper which can shoot out and grab prey. The dragonfly nymph is more robust than that of the damselfly. Gills are in the rectum, and can expel water with such force that the nymph is propelled forward rapidly. About 130 species, 45-140 mm wingspan. ☐ **Naaldekokers**.

Earwigs
(order Dermaptera)

Found in moist places, for instance under stones and in humus. Feed on plant material. Hind wings are large and ear-like, forewings hard and short. Pincers are used to fold hind wings under forewings, and to show aggression. Completely harmless. About 30 species, 8-45 mm.
☐ **Oorkruipers**.

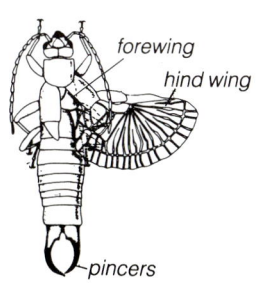

Termites (order Isoptera)

All species are social and live in colonies that range in size from small to very large. One (often very large) queen (a) lays all the eggs, producing workers (b), underdeveloped and sterile males and females that do all the work, and soldiers (c), similarly sterile, whose only function is defence. Reproductive males and females are winged (d) when they leave the nest in swarms to mate and start new colonies. The queen may live for more than 20 years, attended by workers and her male mate, who remains normal in size. When the queen dies, she is replaced by several (smaller) queens.

The soldiers of some species are blind and have a prominent snout or pointed forehead gland (e) from which they squirt a sticky secretion on to their enemies.

Harvester termites and hay-makers gather grass as food for their colonies, and thus cause damage to grazing. While most termites are beneficial as they recycle humus, dead wood and dry manure in the veld, some fungus termites damage wooden structures by chewing up wood to construct 'gardens' on which they grow special fungi for food. Termites are not related to ants. About 200 species, body 3-20 mm (winged adult). □ **Termiete**.

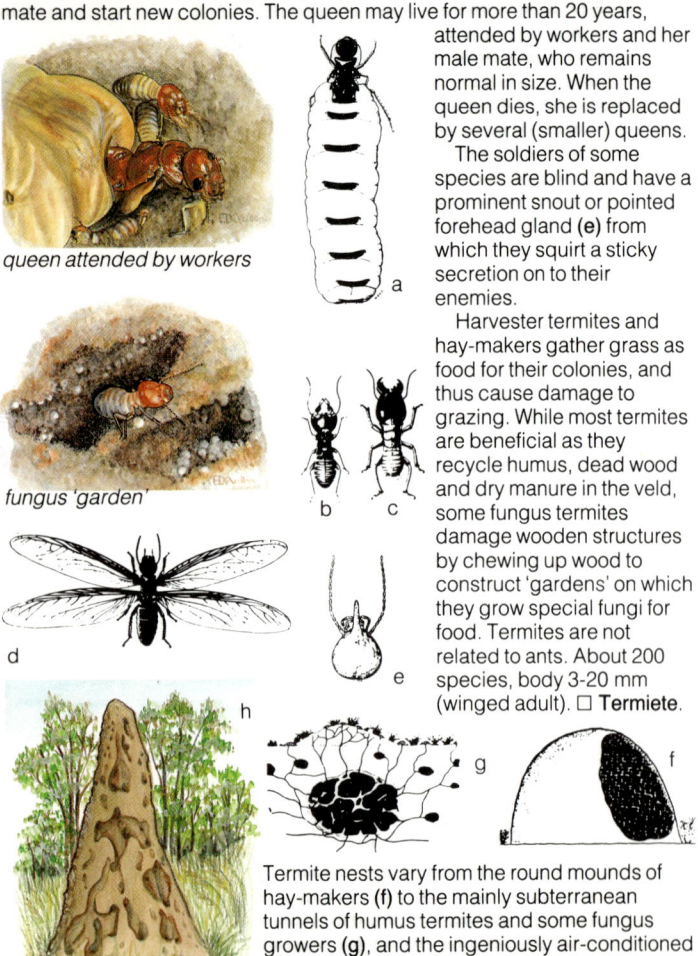

queen attended by workers

fungus 'garden'

Termite nests vary from the round mounds of hay-makers (f) to the mainly subterranean tunnels of humus termites and some fungus growers (g), and the ingeniously air-conditioned high mounds (up to four metres) of the large fungus growers (h). Nests may last for more than 80 years.

Praying mantids
(order Mantodea)

Mantids may be recognized by their front legs (**a**), which are shaped like gin-traps, with sharp spines to grab and hold the insect prey while it is eaten alive; long pronotum (**b**); and cockroach-like wings (**c**).
Mobile head, keen eyesight. Nymph may change appearance drastically with each moult: every stage is adapted to mimic a different background. Plays an important role in Bushman and other ancient folklore. About 120 species, 20-85 mm. □ **Hottentotsgotte**.

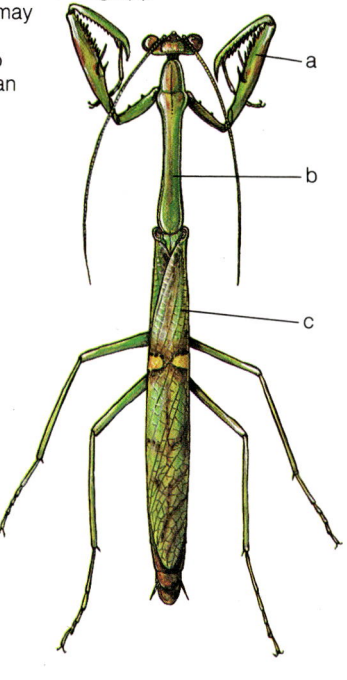

Mantids are always well camouflaged, resembling either leaves, flowers or grasses, as they wait in ambush for their insect prey.

Eggs are laid in a foam mass which congeals and hardens as it is secreted by the female mantid. Some species produce balloon-like egg packets, with the eggs in the middle.

13

Crickets
(order Orthoptera: suborder Ensifera)

The crickets have hind legs adapted for jumping (a), antennae longer than body (b) and their tarsi (feet) have three joints (c). There are two families. The true crickets (Gryllidae) have normal forelegs (d), are omnivorous and very noisy. The male 'chirps' by rubbing his forewings together and using them as concave sound reflectors (e). About 70 species, 10-70 mm.
☐ **Krieke**.

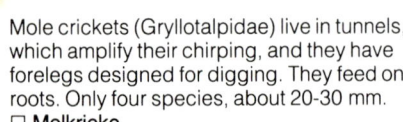

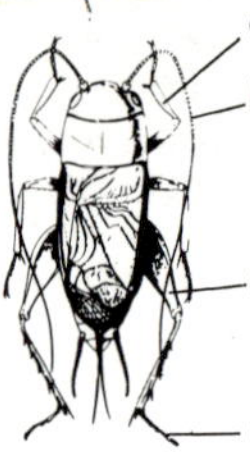

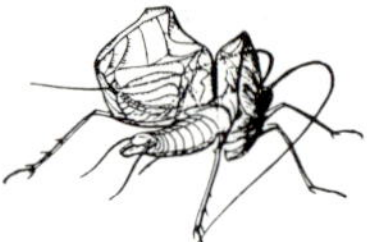

mole cricket in tunnel

Mole crickets (Gryllotalpidae) live in tunnels, which amplify their chirping, and they have forelegs designed for digging. They feed on roots. Only four species, about 20-30 mm.
☐ **Molkrieke**.

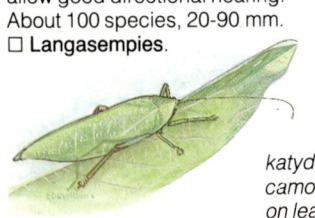

mole cricket's 'digging' foreleg

Katydids
(order Orthoptera: suborder Ensifera)

With their long antennae, katydids resemble crickets but they differ by having four joints on their tarsi (a). Nocturnal. The majority are plant-eaters but some are insect predators. They have cryptic coloration and often resemble leaves. Female has a long ovipositor (egg-laying tube) on her hind body. Male sings (stridulates) loudly with his wings. 'Ears' on the front legs (b) allow good directional hearing. About 100 species, 20-90 mm.
☐ **Langasempies**.

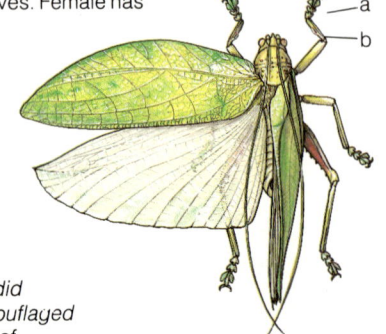

katydid camouflaged on leaf

Locusts and grasshoppers
(order Orthoptera: suborder Caelifera)

These insects are referred to as grasshoppers in the solitary phase, and locusts in the swarm phase. Locusts and grasshoppers often have different colour forms, for instance brown and green specimens can occur within the same species. In swarm locusts, sparse populations initially behave and appear like normal grasshoppers. When densities increase, they become very active and their appearance changes drastically, hoppers becoming brightly coloured and the adults being smaller and long-winged. All grasshoppers and locusts eat only plants. There are about 650 local species, ranging from 10-110 mm. □ **Treksprinkane** en **Sprinkane**.

adult locust

Locusts and grasshoppers have hind legs adapted for jumping (**a**) and antennae shorter than the body (**b**). Their 'ears' are on either side of the first segment of the abdomen (**c**). Females lack the long ovipositor (egg-laying tube) of crickets.

The female locust lays eggs to a depth of 100 mm in the soil using her telescopic abdomen (**d**). Eggs (**e**) hatch, the young hoppers emerge and moult about six times (**f**), the wing-buds getting longer at each stage, until the adult stage is reached.

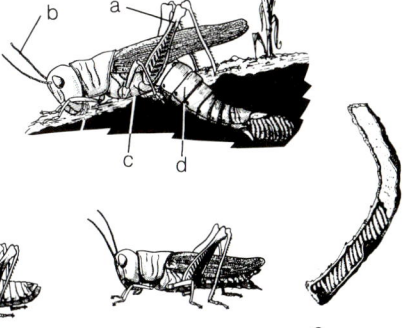

f

e

While swarms of locusts are notorious destroyers of crops, they are also a traditional source of food for indigenous people. Four species of swarm locust occur in southern Africa, and each has a distinct outbreak area (**A**), where swarm densities build up from the solitary phase, a permanent range (**B**) and an invasion area (**C**) where swarms may occasionally invade.

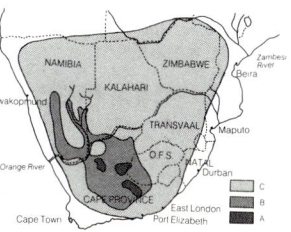

15

Locusts and grasshoppers (cont.)

The common milkweed grasshopper has both winged and wingless adults, and gets its poisonous body fluids from the milkweed on which it feeds.

Many grasshoppers are brightly coloured, warning predators of their poisonous or evil-tasting defence fluids. Some can squirt or produce foam from these secretions when disturbed.

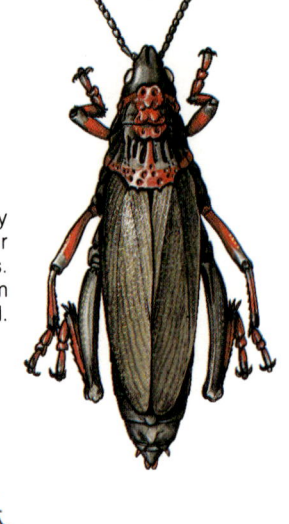

Some grasshoppers, like the crested grasshopper, rely on camouflage for defence, mimicking grasses, leaves or even rocks. They often remain wingless as adults.

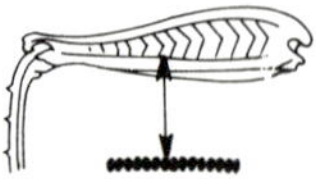

Most grasshoppers stridulate ('sing') by rubbing the file-like serrations on their hind legs against their forewings.

Toad grasshoppers are slow moving, and are mostly nocturnal. Males are often winged, females wingless.

Stick insects
(order Phasmatodea)

With their long, thin bodies and legs, stick insects closely resemble the grasses and twigs on which they rely for camouflage. They vary in length from 10 mm to giants of 250 mm. There are about 50 local species, all plant feeders. Stick insects have some curious properties. They can regrow damaged limbs, and change colour like chameleons. Other methods of defence consist of frightening predators with their brightly coloured hind wings, or acting dead. Their curiously shaped eggs resemble seeds, and are simply dropped to the ground as the female lays them. □ **Stokinsekte**.

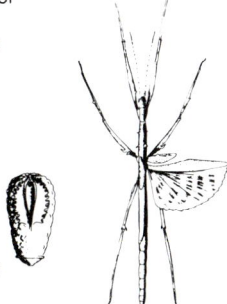

seed-shaped egg

Lice
(order Phthiraptera)

Minute (2-12 mm), flat, wingless parasites of birds and mammals. About 1 100 species. Tarsi (feet) modified into claws to clasp hair or feathers. Some feed on skin scales; others, like human body lice and crab lice, are blood-sucking. Transfer from host to host is always through body contact. □ **Luise**.

Bugs
(order Hemiptera)

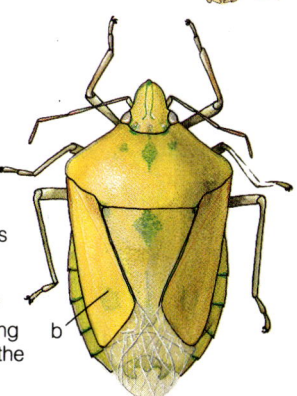

In scientific terms 'bugs' refer to a very large and varied group of insects (about 4 500 species) which are characterized by sucking mouthparts **(a)** without mandibles (jaws). Many are serious pests. All live off either plant juices or blood. The true bugs (suborder Heteroptera) have the bottom half of their forewings hardened **(b)**, and the sucking mouthparts at the front of their heads **(c)**. (For the suborder Homoptera see p. 21.) □ **Besies**.

17

Assassin bugs

(order Hemiptera: suborder Heteroptera: family Reduviidae)

Medium-sized bugs (7-30 mm) that feed on insects which they ambush and then pierce with their sharp snouts. The enzymes which they inject into their prey to digest them also serve as an extremely painful weapon against their enemies. Many of the approximately 400 local species have bright warning coloration.
☐ **Roofwantse**.

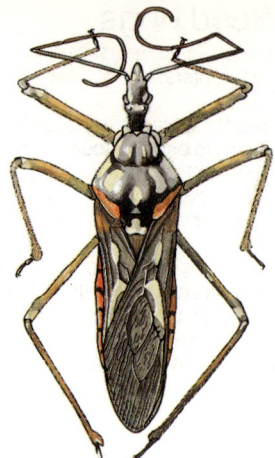

Stainers

(order Hemiptera: suborder Heteroptera: family Pyrrhocoridae)

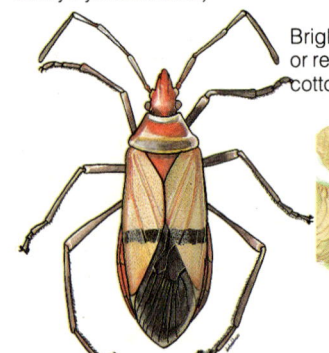

Brightly coloured black and yellow, orange or red bugs. They include pests such as the cotton stainer. Males and females mate tail to tail and may be seen moving about in this position. Differ from the similar-looking seed bugs by lacking ocelli (simple eyes on forehead). Size 5-20 mm, 35 local species.
☐ **Vlekbesies**.

cotton stainers

Bed bugs

(order Hemiptera: suborder Heteroptera: family Cimicidae)

Flat, wingless parasites of humans, birds and bats. Legs normal (see Lice, p. 17). Bed bugs do not live on their hosts, but infest sleeping places, coming out to attack at night. Bed bugs use temperature to locate their hosts, then pierce the skin and suck blood with the rostrum (beak). They can live for months without feeding. Size 4-7 mm, about 10 local species. ☐ **Weeluise**.

Seed bugs

(order Hemiptera: suborder Heteroptera: family Lygaeidae)

Seed bugs range in colour from brown to bright colours, and in size from 2-20 mm. Many species are gregarious and most feed on the juices which they suck from seeds. They resemble stainers, but their forewings have fewer than six veins (stainers have more than seven), and seed bugs usually have ocelli (simple eyes on forehead). About 420 species. □ **Grysbesies**.

forewing has fewer than six veins

Twig wilters

(order Hemiptera: suborder Heteroptera: family Coreidae)

Bugs whose sap-sucking method of feeding often causes twigs to wilt. Both the nymph (immature) and adult can eject a pungent fluid in self-defence. The nymph has its defence gland in the middle of its back, but in the adult the gland is located on the underside near the base of the hind legs, since wings cover the abdomen. Hind legs are often curved and thickened. The oval eggs are laid in groups and, as in all Heteroptera, each egg has a 'lid' through which the young bug emerges. Mostly dull brown, 5-40 mm. About 150 species. □ **Verwelkbesies**.

eggs are laid in groups

detail of egg showing 'lid'

young bug

Shield bugs

(order Hemiptera: suborder Heteroptera: superfamily Pentatomoidea)

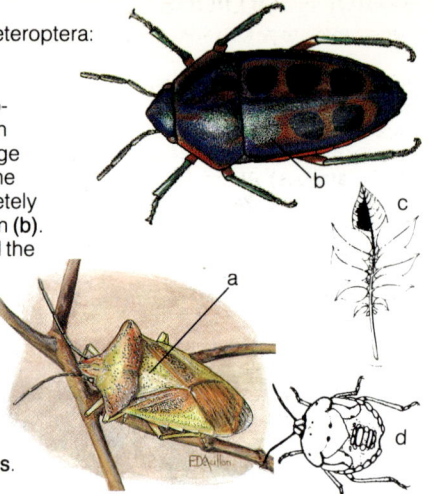

Most shield bugs are plant sap-suckers although some prey on insects. Recognizable by a large triangular shield (a) between the wings: in some cases it completely covers the wings and abdomen (b). Eggs are laid on leaves (c) and the nymphs (d) are characteristically round and brightly coloured. Their defensive secretions are even more evil-smelling than the twig wilters', with the result that they are also known as stink bugs. About 420 species. ☐ **Skildstinkbesies**.

Pond skaters

(order Hemiptera: suborder Heteroptera: family Gerridae)

Slender, agile bugs which run along the surface of the water on their hind and middle legs, using surface tension to stay afloat. They use their front legs to prey on drowning insects. Size 5-20 mm, about 10 species. ☐ **Waterlopers**.

Water bugs

(order Hemiptera: suborder Heteroptera: family Belastomatidae)

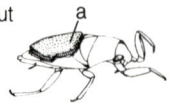

Large (10-75 mm) predacious bugs that live underwater but breathe at the surface through a tube on the tip of the abdomen. Females glue their eggs to wings of males (a). Only four species. ☐ **Reuse waterwantse**.

Back-swimmers

(order Hemiptera: suborder Heteroptera: family Notonectidae)

Small (4-12 mm) water bugs, which characteristically swim on their backs. Prey on small aquatic organisms. About 40 species. ☐ **Rugswemmers**.

Water scorpions
(order Hemiptera: suborder Heteroptera: family Nepidae)

Similar in habits to water bugs, but more sluggish and with a long breathing tube (which, contrary to popular belief, contains no sting and is harmless). About 20-40 mm, three species. ☐ **Waterskerpioene**.

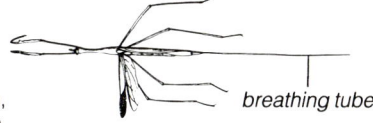
breathing tube

Cicadas
(order Hemiptera: suborder Homoptera: family Cicadidae)

The suborder Homoptera comprises those bugs that have completely membranous wings, and sucking mouthparts situated on the underside of the head. The cicadas are typical examples of this suborder.

Male cicadas use an elaborate sound-producing mechanism to make a very shrill noise to attract females. On either side of the abdomen they have tight membranes and vibrators which produce the sound, while the abdomen itself has air cavities that serve as sound boxes. This whole apparatus is covered with a lid which can direct or muffle the sound. The 140 local cicada species are all sap-suckers. Approximately 10-40 mm long. ☐ **Sonbesies**.

sucking mouthparts

Eggs are laid in branches, which the female pierces with her sharp egg-laying tube. Young nymphs live below ground, feeding on root sap. They may take from two to 17 years to mature. They then surface, creep up plants and shed their strange nymphal skins to become adult cicadas.

adult

nymph

Treehoppers
(order Hemiptera: suborder Homoptera: family Membracidae)

Treehoppers are small (4-8 mm) bugs, often resembling the thorns of their host plant. These 'thorns' or 'horns' are outgrowths of the pronotum (breastplate). Nymphs have a characteristic hairy point on the abdomen and, like the adults, are agile jumpers. About 60 local species. ☐ **Boomspringers**.

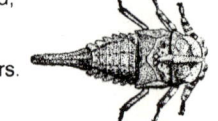

treehopper nymph

Spittle bugs
(order Hemiptera: suborder Homoptera: family Cercopidae)

Medium-sized (6-15 mm) and generally brightly coloured bugs, resembling cicadas (p. 21) but differing by lacking sound organs and having hind legs adapted for jumping. Nymphs produce a frothy foam by blowing air through the honeydew they secrete. This foam or 'cuckoo spit' protects them from desiccation and from being detected and eaten by enemies, and is often produced in such quantities that their host trees drip (so-called 'rain trees').
☐ **Skuimbesies**.

Leafhoppers and lantern bugs
(order Hemiptera: suborder Homoptera: superfamilies Cicadelloidea and Fulgoroidea)

Small (2-30 mm) planthoppers which are found living off the sap of grasses and other plants in our region. Lantern bugs often have curiously elongated heads which may be nearly as long as the rest of the insect. Several are pests, transmitting plant diseases. All are agile jumpers. About 610 species in 21 families in our region. ☐ **Bladspringers** en **lanternbesies**.

Aphids

(order Hemiptera: suborder Homoptera: superfamily Aphidoidea)

Aphids are well-known garden pests. The small (1-6 mm) wingless creatures seen on plants are mostly females which bear live young – without being fertilized by a male. Development is so rapid that unborn females within the mother may already have produced their own young within themselves. Winged males and females are sometimes produced. Aphids excrete prolific amounts of honeydew, which is harvested by ants, and in return for which the ants protect and tend the aphids. About 25 species.
□ **Plantluise**.

Scale insects

(order Hemiptera: suborder Homoptera: families Diaspididae and Coccidae)

Similar to mealy bugs, but the female is either naked or covered by a hard shell. In the hard scale species, eggs (a) hatch under the female's shell and produce active crawlers (b). After moulting, each crawler produces a long thread (c) which it uses to balloon in the wind to another host plant, where it settles and forms a new shell (d). About 400 species. □ **Dopluise**.

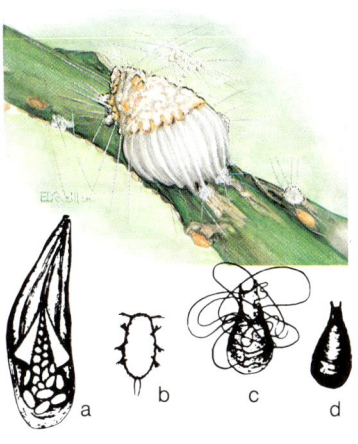

Mealy bugs

(order Hemiptera: suborder Homoptera: family Pseudococcidae)

Mealy bugs do not really look like insects. The female has a small (2-5 mm) sac-like body, often covered with elaborate waxy secretions. These females attach themselves to plants, sucking juice and secreting honeydew. The male is small, with only two wings. About 110 species, many of them pests. □ **Wolluise**.

Antlions (order Neuroptera: family Myrmeleontidae)

Although the adult antlion resembles a dragonfly (see p. 10), it lacks the notch in the front wing margins, and its antennae are long and jointed.

Larvae often live in pits which they construct by excavating holes in sand with their heads and mandibles. These pits serve to trap the ants on which the larvae feed. The larva has neither a mouth nor an anus; the juice of the prey is sucked out through hollow mandibles, and excretions are removed with every moult. There are about 130 species, 13-80 mm.
☐ **Mierleeus**.

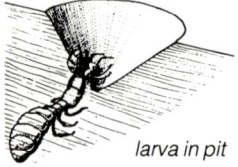
larva in pit

detail of larva

Mantidflies
(order Neuroptera: family Mantispidae)

Mantidflies resemble mantids (see p. 13), but can be distinguished as they have four similar membranous wings (**a**) whereas mantids have leathery forelegs. As in the mantids, forelegs are modified for grabbing prey (**b**). About 35 species, 6-30 mm. ☐ **Valshottentotsgotte**.

Lacewings
(order Neuroptera: family Chrysopidae)

Delicate nocturnal insects. Most of them are green and have very long antennae. Eggs are laid on stalks, and the larvae hunt aphids. About 70 species, 7-30 mm.
☐ **Goudogies**.

Ribbon-winged lacewings
(order Neuroptera: family Nemopteridae)

Similar to lacewings but have long and ribbon- or thread-like hind wings. Larvae are predators and live in sand in caves and rock shelters. Adults pollinate flowers. About 60 species. From 4 mm to more than 100 mm long, including hind wings. ☐ **Lepelvlerkies**.

ribbon-like hind wings

Beetles
(order Coleoptera)

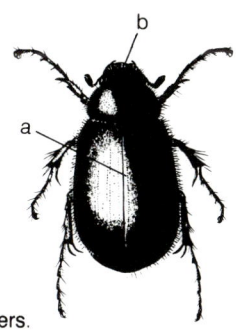

Beetles are by far the largest order of living organisms, and account for more than two-thirds of all insect species. Their main characteristic is that the forewings are hard shells or elytra (a) which cover the thin hind wings used for flying. The only other order in which insects have such wings is that of the earwigs (p. 11), which can be distinguished by their pincers. Some bugs look like beetles, but beetles always have biting mandibles (b) whereas bugs have sucking mouthparts. ☐ Kewers.

Ant beetles
(order Coleoptera: family Paussidae)

These beetles and their larvae live in ant nests as predators of the ants' brood. Ants not only tolerate them, they actually feed them: the elaborate antennae (a) contain glands that secrete a fluid which ants relish. In self-defence the ant beetle can produce a chemical explosion of pungent fluid from a gland on the abdomen. About 150 species, 10-70 mm.
☐ Mierkewers.

Tiger beetles
(order Coleoptera: family Cicindelidae)

Tiger beetles and their larvae are predators of other insects. Larvae live in tunnels and ambush insects that pass within reach. The larva's head fits the tunnel like a lid, while a hook on its back anchors it in the tunnel so that prey cannot drag it out. Tiger beetles are very fast runners, and are usually found in sandy areas near water. Although most fly extremely well and are therefore often confused with flies, some of the large species have no flying wings. About 150 local species, 10-70 mm.
☐ Tierkewers.

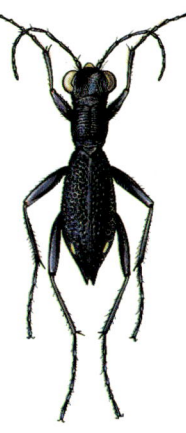

Ground beetles
(order Coleoptera: family Carabidae)

Most ground beetles are good runners but cannot fly. They and their larvae are insect predators. Many species have conspicuous black and red or yellow warning coloration: they can secrete a pungent defensive fluid, either explosively like the ant beetle (p. 25) or squirted at the attacker from a distance. The more than 1 400 local species range from three to 60 mm in length. ☐ **Oogskieters**.

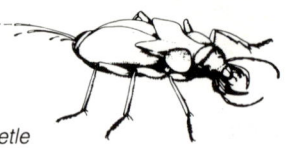

ground beetle squirts defensive fluid

Whirligigs
(order Coleoptera: family Gyrinidae)

Whirligigs float on water, using the surface tension to support them. They have specialized eyes: each eye is divided into an upper part (**a**) for air vision and a lower part (**b**) for water vision. They prey on drowning insects, which they grab with their long forelegs. The other legs are reduced and paddle-like. About 45 species, 3-18 mm.
☐ **Waterhondjies**.

detail of specialized eyes

Water beetles
(order Coleoptera: family Dytiscidae)

Water beetles swim under water, using mainly their long oar-like hind legs. They come to the surface to breathe, and trap an air bubble under the elytra to serve as an aqualung. Like whirligigs, they are streamlined for navigating in water, but both groups can also fly well and move from one lake or stream to another at night. Water beetles' eyes are not divided (**a**). More than 250 local species, 1-25 mm.
☐ **Waterkewers**.   *head detail*

Harlequin beetles
(order Coleoptera: family Histeridae)

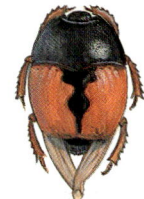

Most of these hard oval beetles are shiny black but some have orange spots. They have strong jaws and feed mainly on maggots, and therefore are usually found under dung pads and in carcasses. A few live with ants or termites as nest parasites. About 100 species, 1-20 mm. ☐ **Harlekynkewers**.

Rove beetles
(order Coleoptera: family Staphylinidae)

Rove beetles have very short elytra (hard forewings) under which they fold their long hind wings, using the flexible abdomen. Most are found in sheltered and moist environments, although many species frequent ant or termite nests. About 750 species, 1-20 mm. ☐ **Kortskildkewers**.

Rhinoceros beetles
(order Coleoptera: family Scarabaeidae: subfamily Dynastinae)

Rhinoceros beetles are large, nocturnal and, like all scarabs, have lamellate antennae. Males of the large species usually have a spectacular horn on the head and pronotum. Larvae are white grubs which live in decaying vegetable matter such as dung or compost heaps. About 60 species, 15-35 mm. ☐ **Renosterkewers**.

lamellate antennae

larva

Stag beetles
(order Coleoptera: family Lucanidae)

Stag beetles have lamellate antennae (**a**) and characteristically large, 'horned' mandibles (**b**). Larvae live in decaying wood. Relatively few (220) species in southern Africa, 15-35 mm. ☐ **Grootkaakkewers**.

Fruit chafers

(order Coleoptera: family Scarabaeidae: subfamily Cetoniinae)

Although some of the most beautiful beetles are to be found in this subfamily, they are not popular with farmers and gardeners as the adults mostly feed on shoots, flowers and fruit. Others feed on honeycombs or wasp nests, or live as ant parasites. The 'goliath' beetles of Africa are the biggest chafers, with our largest local species reaching 70 mm. The smallest of the 160 local species is about 10 mm long. □ **Vrugtetorre**.

Dung beetles

(order Coleoptera: family Scarabaeidae: subfamily Scarabaeinae)

A very large subfamily (about 1 800 local species, 5-50 mm) of diverse appearance and habits. All the larvae are, however, typical white grubs that mostly live off dung. The adults of some species are ballrollers, shaping dung balls out of pads and rolling them away (backwards) to bury and store them as food for themselves or their larval offspring. The flightless dung beetles of the Namib carry dung pellets in their hind legs while running forwards.

While some species simply feed and breed within the dung pad, others dig their tunnels beneath the pad and carry the dung down into their burrows. Larvae always pupate in the soil, and emerge as the adult beetles. □ **Miskruiers**.

ballroller

larva

dung taken down into burrows

Jewel beetles
(order Coleoptera: family Buprestidae)

These torpedo-shaped beetles are usually brightly coloured and shiny. Larvae are woodborers, with a characteristic flattened breast-part (a) that has earned them the misnomer 'flat-headed' borers. Some of the smaller species mine leaves or grass stems. Large, hairy buprestids known as 'brush beetles' occur in the Cape, particularly Namaqualand. Adults are heat-loving and are most active at midday. About 1 200 local species, 1,5-50 mm. □ **Pragkewers**.

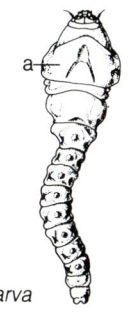

larva

typical flower-visiting jewel beetle

Click beetles
(order Coleoptera: family Elateridae)

Although click beetles resemble jewel beetles in shape, there are two differences. The click beetle's pronotum is always sharply pointed in the rear corners (a), and can tilt up and down. On the underside, the breast-part has a spine (b) which can press on the foremost part of the abdomen, and then click into a groove (c). This mechanism enables the beetle to jerk itself so forcefully that it can right itself from lying on its back or extract itself from a predator's grip. Larvae of some click beetles are known as wireworms and wreak havoc in newly cultivated fields by cutting off young seedlings just below the soil surface. About 700 local species, 4-80 mm. □ **Kniptorre**.

Fireflies
(order Coleoptera: family Lampyridae)

Fireflies produce their light most efficiently, turning it on and off with nerve impulses. Males can fly, whereas females are usually wingless 'glow worms'. The purpose of the light is to enable males and females to find each other. Larvae mostly eat slugs. About 30 species, 5-20 mm. ☐ **Vuurvliegies**.

Flat beetles (order Coleoptera: family Lycidae)

Flat beetles are commonly seen on flowers. They all look rather similar (apart from size), and all are poisonous. Many other beetles, and even moths, wasps and cockroaches mimic the orange and black colour pattern of flat beetles to protect themselves from predators. Larvae are insect predators. About 50 species, 6-22 mm.
☐ **Blaarvlerkkewers**.

Blister beetles or CMR beetles
(order Coleoptera: family Meloidae)

These colourful, soft-bodied beetles are well-known garden pests as the adults feed on flowers. Larvae feed on locust eggs in the soil. All are poisonous. About 350 species, 5-40 mm.
☐ **Blaartrekkewers, CMR-kewers**.

Flower beetles
(order Coleoptera: family Melyridae)

The best-known species is the spotted maize beetle which is often seen in great numbers feeding on the pollen of maize and sunflowers. Flower beetles are poisonous. About 250 species, many of which are metallic green or blue in colour, 5-25 mm. ☐ **Blomkewers**.

Shot-hole borers
(order Coleoptera: family Bostrychidae)

These cylindrical woodborers are usually responsible for the perfectly round holes seen in infested logs and branches. Many species use their mandibles to ringbark branches, and lay their eggs on the dying branch. The larvae then bore into the wood, and the life cycle is completed. Adults fly out to mate and infest new wood. Some species are pests in sapwood and bamboo. About 60 species, 3-30 mm.
☐ **Stompkopboorders**.

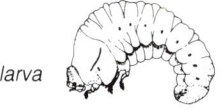
larva

Ladybirds
(order Coleoptera: family Coccinellidae)

Most ladybirds are useful insects, since both larvae and adults feed on aphids (p. 23). Their striking colours are in fact a warning to predators that ladybirds are unpalatable. Larvae of ladybirds are very active predators and, like the adults, are protected by warning coloration and a foul taste.

Some ladybirds, including agricultural pests such as the potato ladybird, feed on plants. Many species hibernate in large swarms, usually settling in rock crevices in the most prominent hills of an area. In autumn, ladybirds from many kilometres around converge on these established hibernation sites. About 250 local species, 0,5-10 mm. ☐ **Skilpadkewers**.

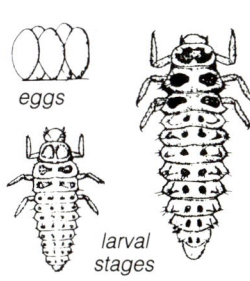
eggs

larval stages

pupa

Darkling or tenebrionid beetles
(order Coleoptera: family Tenebrionidae)

The majority of species in this very varied family are wingless and black or dark grey. Some are fast runners and are active during the day, while others are sluggish and move about only at night or after rain. In South Africa many tenebrionid beetles attract a mate by knocking their abdomens on the ground in a code characteristic of their particular species. This has earned them the colloquial name 'toktokkies'.

Tenebrionid beetles are particularly abundant in the drier parts of the country. In the Namib desert there are hundreds of species, including some with white shells to reflect the desert heat, others with extremely long legs to enable them to run high above the scorchingly hot sand, and some that are discus-shaped which enables them to walk or 'swim' under the sand, cutting through it with the sharp body-edge.

Like the adults, larvae feed mostly on plant litter. They are relatively hard, shiny and smooth. About 3 200 local species, 2-65 mm. □ **Toktokkies**.

typical tenebrionid beetle

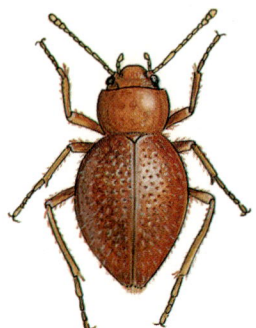

nocturnal Namib species

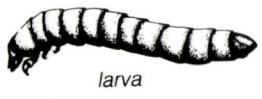

larva

'toktokkie' knocking

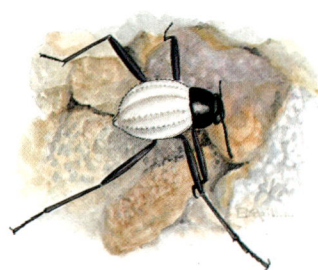

some desert species have long legs to enable them to run high above the hot sand

Longicorns

(order Coleoptera: family Cerambycidae)

Longicorns are woodborers, and are recognizable by their extended antennae. Their life cycle is very long: from three to eight years is not unusual, but large species may take up to 20 years to reach maturity. This is because the dry wood on which the larvae feed is very low in nutrient value.

brightly coloured diurnal species

longicorn showing very long antennae

The larvae are similar to those of the jewel beetles (p. 29), but are not flattened behind the head. When they pupate in the dead wood (usually in the roots), some species line the pupal cell with calcrete which they secrete. In South West Africa these calcrete shells are often found in the veld because they last longer than the soft wood of their succulent host plants. They are then usually mistaken for eggshells.

larva

nocturnal species are usually less colourful

Adult longicorns are among the most beautiful and colourful of insects, particularly the diurnal species which are often found feeding on flowers or chewing bark off branches. Nocturnal species are usually duller. Virtually all species can stridulate by rubbing the pronotum against the back. About 650 species, from 3 mm to giants of up to 100 mm. ☐ **Boktorre**.

Leaf beetles
(order Coleoptera: family Chrysomelidae: subfamily Eumolpinae)

Most leaf beetles are brightly and beautifully coloured. The adults and larvae both feed on the leaves of the same host plant. Larvae are slug-like, often covered with slime. Many species' larvae stick debris from their environment – including their own excrement – on to this slime to make themselves inconspicuous and unpalatable to their enemies. About 175 local species (but more than 1 500 in the whole family), 2-15 mm. ☐ **Blaarvreetkewers**.

Tortoise beetles (order Coleoptera: family Chrysomelidae: subfamily Cassidinae)

These pretty tortoise-shaped beetles are also known as 'fool's gold' beetles because of their lustrous colours which are reflections of the tissue below the translucent shell. This lustre fades after death. The larva has a spiny 'tail' on which it collects the crumpled skins of its various moults, and which it then carries above itself like an umbrella (**a**). About 90 species, 5-20 mm. ☐ **Klatergoudkewers**.

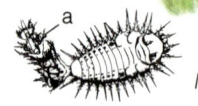

larva

Leaf-mining beetles
(order Coleoptera: family Chrysomelidae: subfamily Hispinae)

The curious spiny appearance of these small beetles is probably an adaptation to their unusual environment. The larva feeds and pupates between the upper and lower 'skins' of a leaf. The adult eventually emerges from this thin-walled cavity. About 125 species, 1-10 mm.
☐ **Blaarmynkewers**.

Weevils

(order Coleoptera: family Curculionidae)

The weevils or snouted beetles are the largest beetle family, with over 2 500 species in southern Africa, and range from 1-60 mm in length. The head is always elongated to a greater or lesser degree between the eyes and the mandibles in front.

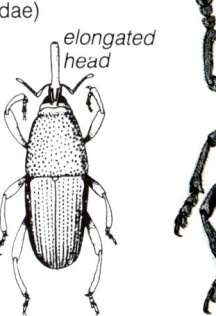
elongated head

The female cycad weevil uses her extremely long snout to bore through the protective layer of dead leaves around the stem of the cycad, and into the stem. She then lays an egg, and uses her snout to push the egg down to the bottom of this tunnel. The larva starts feeding there.

The leaf-rolling weevil cuts leaves in a precise pattern, then rolls and folds the excised piece between its legs until it has a

female cycad weevil

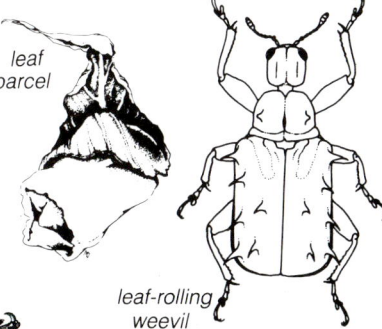

leaf parcel

leaf-rolling weevil

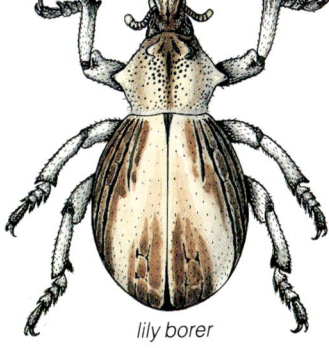

lily borer

neat leaf-parcel. This parcel contains its egg and serves as both protection and food for the larva. All weevil larvae are legless.

Weevils are plant feeders and, depending on the species, eat anything from roots to seeds. As a result many, such as the granary weevil, are agricultural pests. Some of the large, wingless lily borers may live for as long as 30 years.
□ **Snuitkewers.**

35

Flies and mosquitoes
(order Diptera)

This order includes all the flies, blowflies, mosquitoes and gnats. They all have a pair of large membranous wings (**a**), a second pair of wings reduced to halteres (**b**), thorax usually large and rounded (**c**), and sucking or licking mouthparts (**d**) used to lick or to pierce plants or animals' skin to feed on sap or blood. Larvae are legless and are known as maggots. More than 5 300 species are found in South Africa. ☐ **Tweevlerkiges**.

Mosquitoes
(order Diptera: suborder Nematocera: family Culicidae)

Mosquitoes usually feed on plant sap but the females also feed on the blood of humans, other vertebrates and even insects. The male (which never feeds on blood) has feather-shaped antennae to receive the buzzing of the female. The female lays her eggs on water and the larvae and pupae live in water. Mosquitoes carry and transmit diseases such as malaria and yellow fever. About 133 species, 4-10 mm. ☐ **Muskiete**.

larva

Crane flies
(order Diptera: suborder Nematocera: family Tipulidae)

larva

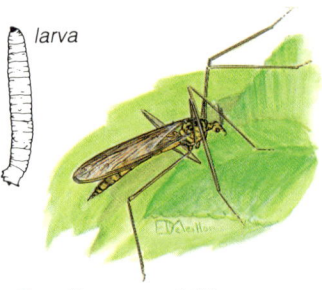

Large (10-25 mm) insects, resembling hanging flies, but having only two wings. Legs are extremely long. Adults apparently never eat. Larvae live in water or moist soil, adults in dense vegetation. About 250 species. ☐ **Langbeenmuskiete**.

Stalk-eyed flies
(order Diptera: suborder Cyclorrhapha: family Diopsidae)

Characterized by having immobile eyes on stalks on either side of the head, almost as if the fly has an extra pair of long feelers. The reason for the eyestalks is unknown. 33 species, 5-15 mm. ☐ **Steeloogvlieë**.

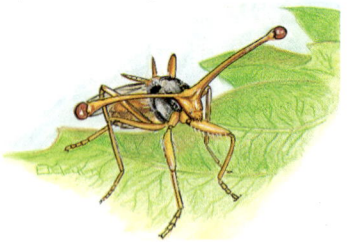

Flies (order Diptera: suborder Cyclorrhapha: family Muscidae)

Common flies, such as the house fly, are 5-10 mm long and there are 364 local species. The majority of the adults use the proboscis ('tongue') to lick up food while others, for example the stable fly, are blood suckers. Larvae are all typical maggots that live on dung and other decomposing material. Flies are carriers of diseases such as dysentery. ☐ **Vlieë**.

Horse flies (order Diptera: suborder Brachycera: family Tabanidae)

As in the case of the mosquito, the females are blood suckers while the males feed on nectar. The females can ingest large amounts of blood and are carriers of various human and animal diseases. Eggs are laid near or in damp soil. Larvae are usually found underground and are insect predators or, occasionally, herbivores. About 10-25 mm, 227 species. ☐ **Blindevlieë**.

Blowflies (order Diptera: suborder Cyclorrhapha: family Calliphoridae)

Stoutly built flies, usually metallic green or blue. These flies are well-known for the harm they do to sheep: they lay their eggs in wet wool or in open wounds on the sheep, and the maggots bore into the flesh where they live and feed. Just before the pupal stage, they drop to the ground and bury themselves. They emerge as adults. About 6-15 mm, 145 species. ☐ **Skaapbrommers**.

maggot

Fruit flies (order Diptera: suborder Cyclorrhapha: family Tephritidae)

Fruit flies have conspicuously patterned wings. A pest of most fruits and also of some vegetables such as pumpkins, the fruit fly lays its eggs under the peel and the maggots live and feed inside the fruit before dropping to the ground and pupating in the soil. The adults feed on nectar. About 4-8 mm, 375 species. ☐ **Vrugtevlieë**.

Robber flies
(order Diptera: suborder Brachycera: family Asilidae)

Adults use their strong spiny legs to catch insects in flight. They then find a suitable perch and, with their sharp mouthparts, suck the body fluid from their prey. Females lay eggs in or on the ground or on plants. The maggots are herbivores and live in the ground or inside plant tissue. About 500 local species, 3-40 mm. ☐ **Roofvlieë**.

Bee flies
(order Diptera: suborder Brachycera: family Bombyliidae)

The adults feed on nectar sucked through a long proboscis. When in flight they can characteristically 'hang' in the air, and the females use this ability to shoot their eggs into the tunnels of other insects. The maggots, which are parasitic on the eggs and larvae of other insects such as digger wasps (p. 46), pupate just below the soil surface. 940 local species, 3-30 mm. ☐ **Byvlieë**.

Red-headed flies
(order Diptera: suborder Cyclorrhapha: family Platystomatidae)

These flies have obvious warning coloration and taste foul. Adult flies feed on any decomposing liquid as well as nectar. Larvae feed on rotting organic material. About 80 local species, 10-30 mm. ☐ **Rooikopvlieë**.

Louse flies
(order Diptera: suborder Cyclorrhapha: family Hippoboscidae)

All the adults are external, blood-sucking parasites of mammals and birds. Some species are wingless. Females are viviparous and give birth to one maggot just before it pupates. The flies also apparently transport other parasites, such as lice, from one host to another. 37 local species, 6-15 mm. ☐ **Luisvlieë**.

Butterflies and moths
(order Lepidoptera)

Butterflies and moths are easily recognizable by their four large, scale-covered wings. They usually have two prominent 'mouth feelers' apart from the ordinary feelers or antennae (a) and a long, rolled-up proboscis or 'tongue' (b). Butterflies are always diurnal, whereas the majority of moths fly only at night. A butterfly's antennae are always clubbed. Larvae of both moths and butterflies are known as caterpillars. About 10 000 species, ranging from 3-180 mm in wingspan, occur in South Africa. ☐ **Skoenlappers** en **motte**.

Blues and coppers
(order Lepidoptera: family Lycaenidae)

Mostly metallic blue and copper brown butterflies. They often have eyemarks and 'tails' on the rear margin of the hind wings. The butterfly sits with its wings folded and touching above the body with the result that the 'tails' look like feelers – an illusion enhanced when the butterfly moves. Predators that try to grab the butterfly by the 'head' only break off pieces of the wing ('tails'). Caterpillars usually associate with ants which tend and feed them; in turn, they secrete a substance relished by the ants. Wingspan 10-50 mm, 281 species. ☐ **Bloutjies** en **kopertjies**.

Monarchs (order Lepidoptera: family Danaidae)

The body fluid of the monarchs is poisonous because the milkweed plants on which the caterpillars feed are poisonous. Many other butterflies mimic the warning coloration of the monarchs. Before pupating, the caterpillar spins a silken thread which it attaches to the plant. The caterpillar, and in turn the pupa, hangs from it. Wingspan about 40-60 mm, 7 species. ☐ **Melkbosskoenlappers**.

pupa

Whites
(order Lepidoptera: family Pieridae)

Mostly white and yellow butterflies with rounded wings. Some species migrate in large swarms in summer. The caterpillars of various species are pests on cabbage and lucerne. The eggs have a characteristic complex of surface ridges. About 53 species, wingspan up to 50 mm. ☐ **Witjies**.

Reds (order Lepidoptera: family Acraeidae)

Poisonous or bad-tasting butterflies. When in danger, the adults can secrete a poisonous fluid. Their warning colours are often mimicked by other butterflies. Wingspan about 30 mm, 56 species.
☐ **Rooitjies**.

Swallowtails
(order Lepidoptera: family Papilionidae)

Large (wingspan 50-100 mm) butterflies of which the best known is the citrus swallowtail. Many of the females mimic poisonous butterflies and do not resemble the male. Early instar caterpillars mimic bird droppings while later instars are camouflaged green and white on leaves. 17 species. ☐ **Swaelsterte**.

Swifts (order Lepidoptera: family Charaxidae)

Large butterflies (wingspan 40-60 mm). Fast flyers with characteristic 'tails' on the hind wings. The adults do not feed on nectar as other butterflies do, but suck the fluid from decomposing material or predator dung. 36 species. ☐ **Dubbelsterte**.

Nymphalid butterflies
(order Lepidoptera: family Nymphalidae)

Medium to large butterflies (wingspan 30-60 mm), which often mimic poisonous butterflies such as the reds. Adults are usually seen perching with their wings extended. The female lays her eggs on an appropriate plant; the caterpillars feed on the plant and moult several times. Before pupating, the caterpillar spins a silk thread on to a branch, and uses it to hang upside-down from the tip of its abdomen. It pupates in this position. Adults feed on nectar. 70 species. ☐ **Borselpootskoenlappers**.

Emperor moths
(order Lepidoptera: family Saturniidae)

Large moths (wingspan 180 mm). Females lay eggs in clusters on the food plant of the larvae. On hatching, caterpillars eat the eggshells before beginning to eat plant leaves. Caterpillars have fleshy protuberances and are usually brightly coloured (for example, the mopane worm). In large numbers the caterpillars are capable of defoliating trees and therefore may be pests in plantations. Caterpillars of most species pupate in the ground.

The male moths have large feathered antennae which they use to smell the 'perfume' or pheromone which the females emit. Males can be collected easily by placing a freshly

mopane worm

female

male

feathered antennae

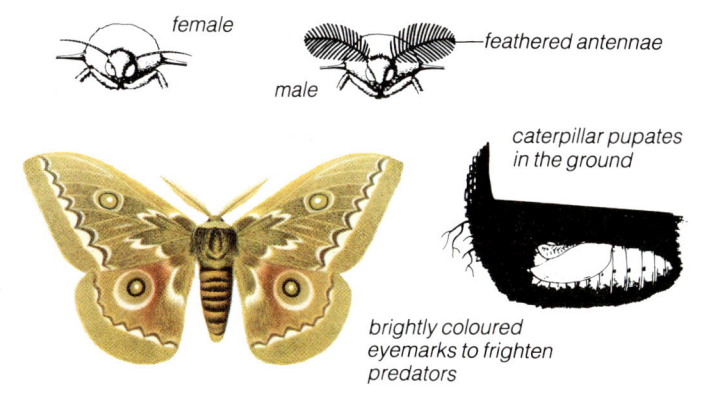

caterpillar pupates in the ground

brightly coloured eyemarks to frighten predators

emerged, unmated female in a cage in the vicinity of the males.

The emperor moth is usually active only at night: during the day it can be found resting on tree trunks. When in danger it jerks its front wings forward to expose the hind wings which have large, brightly coloured eyemarks to frighten predators.

The majority of the 65 local species occur in the forest areas of the eastern Transvaal and Natal. While some species are abundant, a few are exceptionally rare and confined to small areas. ☐ **Pou-oogmotte**.

Hawk moths (order Lepidoptera: family Sphingidae)

The hawk moth is large (wingspan 35-100 mm) and a very fast flyer with a streamlined body and pointed abdomen. The adult feeds on nectar, usually at dusk, and can be seen hovering above flowers, probing them with its long proboscis.

The caterpillar is smooth-bodied and has a pointed 'tail'. Some have large eyemarks on the breast-part while others have oblique stripes down the sides of the body. They pupate either in the soil or in thin silken cocoons among dried leaf litter.

Forewings are large and triangular, hind wings are small. The 'death's head' hawk moth steals honey from beehives, and is known to migrate long distances (in Europe, it crosses the Alps) in search of the larvae's food plants in order to lay its eggs.

The proboscis (a) is usually longer than the moth's body. However, the 'death's head' hawk moth has a shorter proboscis which it uses to make a high-pitched noise by swallowing air and then forcing it out through the proboscis. About 100 local species. ☐ **Pylstertmotte**.

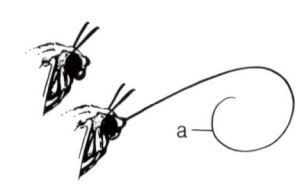

Owl moths
(order Lepidoptera: family Noctuidae)

Mostly inconspicuous grey moths which are active at night. Adults usually feed on nectar, but some feed on fruit or even the eye-moisture of animals.

Eggs are laid on the food plant of the caterpillar. Caterpillars are herbivores and many are serious agricultural pests (for example, cutworms, commando worms, stem borers and bollworms). Wingspan 15-100 mm, about 1 700 species. ☐ **Uilmotte**.

larva

Bagworms
(order Lepidoptera: family Psychidae)

Only the male bagworm has wings (wingspan approx. 30 mm). The female lives permanently in the bag of sticks, grass, thorns, leaves or even stones which the larva constructs and binds together with silk. The male mates with the female through the opening in the bag, and she then lays her eggs inside the bag. Caterpillars hatch, eat the remains of the female, then leave the bag and disperse by spinning long silken threads on which they hang from the branches. The wind disperses each caterpillar on its 'parachute' to another food plant where it constructs a new 'house' which it gradually enlarges. The caterpillar pupates inside the bag. About 30 species. □ **Sakwurms**.

(Left to right) The female lives in a bag of sticks, grass, thorns, leaves or even stones.

Day-flying moths
(order Lepidoptera: family Zygaenidae)

Small moths (wingspan 20-50 mm), mostly brightly coloured as a warning: the majority are poisonous because the larvae feed on poisonous plants. Adults fly during the day and feed on nectar. About 100 species. □ **Dagvlieënde motte**.

Woolly bears
(order Lepidoptera: family Eupterotidae)

Wingspan 30-120 mm. The adult moths are nocturnal, and are hairy. Larvae have short poisonous spines and long soft 'hair' which they weave into the cocoon while pupating. Caterpillars eat grass, adults are nectar feeders. About 100 species. □ **Wolhaarruspes**.

larva

43

Loopers
(order Lepidoptera: family Geometridae)

looper caterpillar

Small to large (wingspan 10-60 mm) yellow or green moths. The hind and forewings are similar in shape. Caterpillars, known as 'loopers', generally have two pairs of legs on the abdomen and the usual six on the thorax. They move by looping the body, bringing the hind legs up to the forelegs, and then straighten out by moving the forelegs forward. More than 1 000 local species. ☐ **Landmeters**.

Wasps, bees and ants
(order Hymenoptera)

All members of this group have four membranous wings (a) (if they are winged), the thorax and abdomen joined by means of a petiole (b), and mouthparts with mandibles (jaws) (c). The majority have a sting (d), originally the female's ovipositor. About 6 000 species. ☐ **Vliesvlerke**.

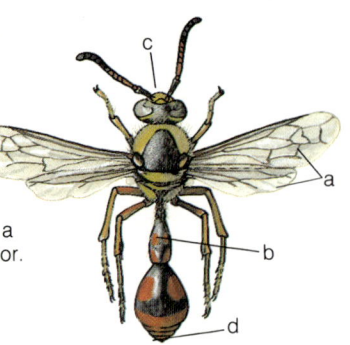

Parasitic wasps
(order Hymenoptera: superfamilies Chalcidoidea and Ichneumonoidea)

The female parasitic wasp uses her ovipositor to lay eggs in or on her insect host. The hatched larvae then feed on the host. The wood-boring parasitic wasp can hear and smell her host through as much as 30 mm of wood and will use her ovipositor to bore until contact is made with the host.

The majority are parasitic on insect eggs and are therefore exceptionally small (0,2-3 mm). However, those that parasitize adult insects or larvae may be as large as 60 mm.
☐ **Parasietwespes**.

typical parasitic wasp

female boring into wood

Cuckoo wasps
(order Hymenoptera: family Chrysididae)

Beautiful metallic green, blue or purple wasps with exceptionally hard armour. They have the ability to roll themselves into a hard ball: a necessary form of protection as they lay eggs in the nests of mud wasps and spider wasps. The cuckoo wasp larva (a) feeds on the host larva and its food supply (b). About 5-20 mm, 220 species. ☐ **Koekoekwespes**.

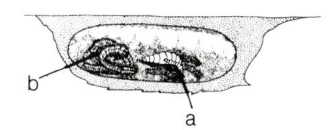

Velvet ants
(order Hymenoptera: family Mutillidae)

Velvet ants are in fact wingless wasps which, like the cuckoo wasps, lay their eggs in the nests of solitary bees and wasps. They are red and black with white dots and have a very hard body armour. Can inflict a painful sting. Males are winged and often carry females through the air while mating. About 200 species, 2-30 mm. ☐ **Fluweelmiere**.

Spider wasps
(order Hymenoptera: family Pompilidae)

These wasps hunt spiders exclusively. Following a dramatic fight, the wasp paralyzes the spider by stinging it accurately in a specific nerve centre. The spider, which will be food for the hatched larva, is then buried with a wasp egg. More than 200 species, 5-70 mm. ☐ **Spinnekopjagters**.

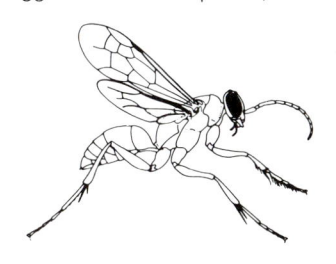

Mud wasps and digger wasps
(order Hymenoptera: family Sphecidae)

Small to large wasps (1-45 mm) which build nests either from gathered mud or by digging holes in the ground. The wasp lays its egg, then provides paralyzed insects or larvae for the larva to eat once it hatches. About 740 species. ☐ **Kleiwespes** en **graafwespes**.

Paper wasps
(order Hymenoptera: family Vespidae)

Differ from other wasps in that their forewings are folded longitudinally when at rest, reducing them to half their normal width. Some species, for example the bee pirate, build nests similar to those of the digger wasps, while others live socially and build large paper nests.

The large paper wasps use finely chewed tree bark to build their nests which are commonly found under roof trusses. There is a hierarchy among the females which allows the 'queen' or highest individual to produce most of the eggs, while the lowest-ranking individuals lay practically no eggs and do most of the work.

The larvae of paper wasps are fed progressively with nectar, pollen and finely chewed worms and insects. In winter the mated female wasps hibernate in any sheltered place and thus give up their nests. In summer they return to build new nests. About 35 species, 7-35 mm. ☐ **Perdebye**.

paper nest

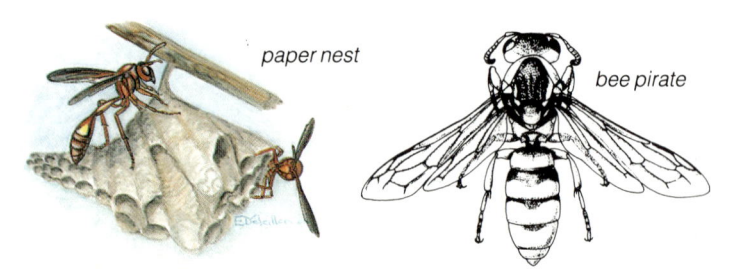

bee pirate

Potter wasps
(order Hymenoptera: family Eumenidae)

These solitary wasps build neat clay pots attached to twigs, grasses or stones. Like the mud wasp, the potter wasp only once provides her eggs in the nests with food.
☐ **Pottebakkerwespes, graafwespes**.

Honey bees
(order Hymenoptera: family Apidae)

This family includes the common honey bee as well as a few wild bee species. All are nectar and pollen feeders and live in social colonies with a single queen. The pollen baskets on the hind legs are characteristic of the honey bees, as are the wax secretions that they use to build their honeycombs.

Mopane bees are small (2 mm) and, like mocca bees, do not have stings. Instead of combs, mocca bees build round wax pots for their honey.
☐ **Bye**.

honey bee

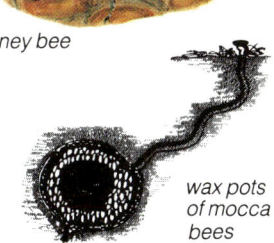

wax pots of mocca bees

Solitary bees
(order Hymenoptera: family Halictidae)

These bees build underground tunnels. Occasionally a group of females will work together, but without any hierarchy ('pecking order'). Larvae are provided at the outset with sufficient pollen and nectar for their needs. A few species are parasites on other solitary bees. About 70 species, 2-15 mm. ☐ **Alleenloperbye**.

Leafcutter bees
(order Hymenoptera: family Megachilidae)

These bees have pollen baskets on the underside of the abdomen. The majority build nests from pieces of leaves, which they neatly cut out in semi-circular shapes. Any appropriate places, such as deserted insect nests, reeds or woodborer tunnels, are used for their tunnels. About 200 species, 3-22 mm.
☐ **Blaarsnyerbye**.

Carpenter bees
(order Hymenoptera:family Anthophoridae: subfamily Xylocopinae)

Carpenter bees are relatively large (10-35 mm). They are wood tunnellers and damage untreated timber, but do not, however, eat the wood. Although they live communally, each female provides her own progeny with nectar and pollen. About 100 species.
☐ **Houtkapperbye**.

Ants
(order Hymenoptera: family Formicidae)

Ants are the most advanced social insects. Apart from the queen, there are various worker and soldier castes, each of which has a specific function. Initially the queen and male are winged and fly out to mate, after which the male dies. The female starts a nest, sheds her wings and lays eggs. All the workers and soldiers are sterile, unwinged females.
 Weaver ants use the silk spun by their larvae to join leaves and so form the nest.
 Ants often tend aphids and social insects to obtain the sweet honeydew they produce. Underground nests are built and organized with chambers for food storage, refuse and incubation. About 600 local species, 1-20 mm.
☐ **Miere**.

Worker ants have characteristically angled antennae.

When making their nests, weaver ants use silk spun by their larvae.

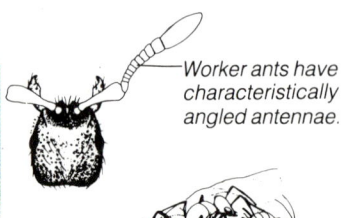

Ants tend aphids to obtain the honeydew they produce.

Some inconspicuous insects

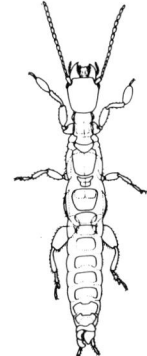

Web spinners
(order Embiidina)

Small to medium-sized (5-25 mm) winged or wingless insects which live in colonies in silk-lined tunnels under rocks or bark. Their thick front tarsi contain the silk glands. Can run equally well forwards or backwards. About 37 species. ☐ **Tonnelspinners**.

Stoneflies
(order Plecoptera)

Small to medium-sized (5-25 mm) insects that resemble cockroaches. Larvae live in water and their shed skins ('shucks') may be found on rocks near streams. Adults have four similar wings, unlike roaches which have leathery forewings. About 20 species. ☐ **Pêrelvlieë**.

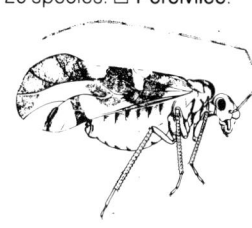

Booklice
(order Psocoptera)

Small (1-10 mm) insects with very long antennae, wings folded roof-like over the body. Head has a bulging 'forehead'. Feed mainly on fungi, but some damage books by eating the bindings. About 80 species. ☐ **Boekluise**.

Alderflies
(order Megaloptera)

Occur only in the Cape and Natal mountains (7 species). Larvae live in water. Adults resemble antlions, but lack forked wing veins (see p. 8). Wingspan 36-80 mm. ☐ **Kameelnekvlieë**.

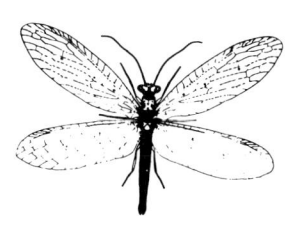

Thrips
(order Thysanoptera)

Small (mostly less than 2 mm), slender insects, many of which are pests. Winged species have the wings fringed with long hairs. Last tarsal segment is bulb-like, face is asymmetrical. About 230 species.
□ **Blaaspootjies**.

Fleas
(order Siphonaptera)

Small (mostly less than 2 mm) blood-sucking mammal parasites. Always wingless and laterally flattened. Can jump more than 100 times their own length. Larvae live off dust, adults can survive without food for up to four months. Notorious as carriers of bubonic plague. About 100 species. □ **Vlooie**.

Caddisflies
(order Trichoptera)

Larvae live under water in cases which they construct from silk and other materials. Adults look and behave like moths, but have very long antennae (a), and hairs instead of scales on their wings. More than 200 species, 3-28 mm. □ **Watermotte**.

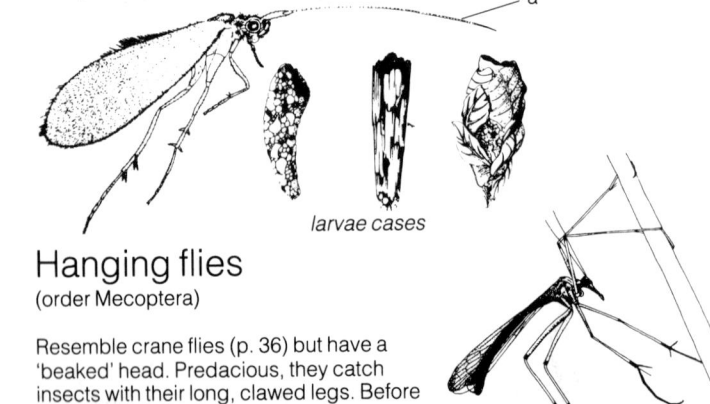

larvae cases

Hanging flies
(order Mecoptera)

Resemble crane flies (p. 36) but have a 'beaked' head. Predacious, they catch insects with their long, clawed legs. Before mating, the male offers a prey item to the female. Size 20-40 mm, 31 species, all from the south-western Cape. □ **Hangvlieë**.

Life cycles

Insects have a curious property in that they change in habits and appearance as they grow. This is called metamorphosis. There are several stages through which an insect may metamorphose, such as from egg to larva to pupa to adult. The three main patterns of metamorphosis and the orders in which they occur are discussed below.

There are two reasons for metamorphosis in insects. Firstly, insects have a more or less hardened cuticle around their bodies, which serves as both skin and skeleton. Since this cuticle cannot grow as the insect grows, it must be shed and replaced by a larger one. A larger cuticle, however, may also require modifications to work efficiently, and this is one reason why insects change as they grow. The second reason is that insects often switch to other food sources as they grow, and these changes require different legs, mouthparts, etc. Where metamorphosis becomes so extreme, it has the advantage that adults do not compete with their offspring for food and space. Not surprisingly, these insects are the most successful and abundant.

Ametabolic life cycle

This is found in fishmoths (order Thysanura), where the young that hatch from the eggs look rather like miniature versions of the adults, and moult several times without changing much until the adult stage is reached.

Life cycle of a fishmoth

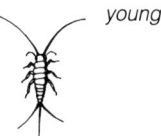

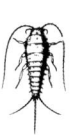

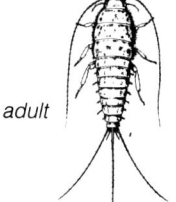

egg *young* *adult*

Hemimetabolic life cycle

In this type of cycle we find eggs, nymphs and adults, but no pupae. Nymphs may more or less resemble the adults in appearance and lifestyle. This situation is found in cockroaches (order Blattodea), termites (Isoptera), praying mantids (Mantodea), earwigs (Dermaptera), web-spinners (Embiidina), crickets and locusts (Orthoptera), stick insects (Phasmatodea), booklice (Psocoptera), lice (Phthiraptera), bugs (Hemiptera) and thrips (Thysanoptera).

Life cycle of a grasshopper

eggs *nymphs* *adult*

Another form of hemimetabolic life cycle is found in those insects which develop from egg to nymph to adult, but in which the nymphal stages do not resemble the adults and live very differently from them. This occurs in those orders where nymphs live in water, but the adults are flying land insects such as mayflies (order Ephemeroptera), dragonflies and damselflies (Odonata), and stoneflies (Plecoptera).

Life cycle of a dragonfly

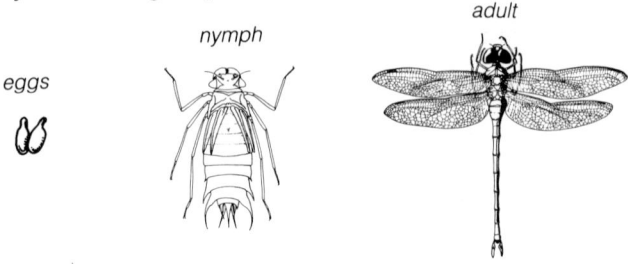

eggs

nymph

adult

Holometabolic life cycle

A life cycle denoted by the stages of egg, larva (which differs drastically from the adult), pupa and, eventually, adult. This cycle occurs in alderflies (order Megaloptera), antlions and lacewings (Neuroptera), beetles (Coleoptera), hanging flies (Mecoptera), flies and mosquitoes (Diptera), fleas (Siphonaptera), caddisflies (Trichoptera), butterflies and moths (Lepidoptera), and wasps, bees and ants (Hymenoptera).

Life cycle of a ladybird

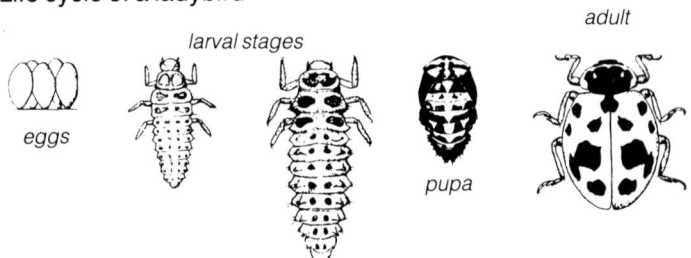

eggs

larval stages

pupa

adult

Some life cycles (for instance, those of aphids and some cockroaches) appear unusual because eggs hatch in the mother, and larvae or nymphs are born. In other cases (such as in some flies) the larvae may even develop and form pupae within the mother, and are then born as complete adults. Yet these insects all follow the standard patterns of metamorphosis before they are born.

Collecting and breeding insects

Making a worthwhile insect collection need not necessarily be expensive. It is, however, important to follow the correct procedures from the beginning, or your efforts will soon be wasted.

Equipment
Before going into the field you must decide whether you want to hunt, research, or collect insects. For insect collecting, wear a practical outfit with many pockets, a hat as protection against the sun, and long trousers as a barrier against thorns and ticks.

You will also need:
1. A few bottles containing 70% alcohol for soft-bodied specimens, for example larvae and termites. Never put delicate-winged insects such as wasps or butterflies in alcohol because their wings will soften and shrivel when mounted dry.
2. A killing bottle with a wide neck and screw top is also required. A piece of tissue paper is placed in the bottle and occasionally dampened with ethyl acetate (best carried in its own small glass container). The killing bottle is then ready to receive captured insects, which die quickly and painlessly by this method. Do not put large beetles and delicate insects together in the bottle as the beetles will almost certainly damage the others.
3. An aspirator is used to pick up very small and delicate insects. It can be made from an old pill bottle, a cork, and two rubber hoses with inner diameters of approximately 5 mm. Two thin glass tubes are inserted through holes in the cork and a piece of fine gauze is attached with an elastic band to the end of one of the glass tubes where it protrudes below the stopper. By sucking on the rubber hose attached to this glass tube, small insects can be drawn up the other rubber hose and into the bottle.
4. Tweezers are practical for handling small insects. A fine, delicate pair of tweezers can be made from a piece of watch spring. Two pieces can be soldered together and the points sharpened on a grinding stone. Alternatively, the springs can be attached at the back by first being heated to soften them, and then being fastened with small rivets.

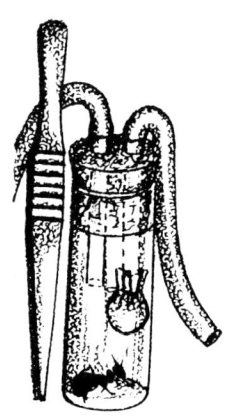

5. A net is essential for collecting flying insects. The frame of a trout net is ideal and the bag can be made from chiffon, as shown in the sketch. For collecting water insects a material with wider mesh is needed to allow more water to pass through. When 'sweeping' insects from grass and trees a net with a sturdy frame and handle is required.

Collecting in soil
Many insects, such as dung beetles, tunnel underground and an effective way to locate them is to dig along their tunnels. Digger wasps usually carry paralyzed but otherwise undamaged insects (caterpillars, beetles or grasshoppers, depending on the wasp species) into their nests. By observing the nests and then digging them up, you can collect many perfect specimens. Ant and termite nests always have to be dug open in order to collect these insects and their parasites. Beware of scorpions' flat tunnels!

Collecting on ground level
A large variety of insects live under stones, on the ground or in humus. One of the easiest ways to collect these insects is to bury a tin or bottle with its opening level with the ground. A funnel opening into a bottle containing 70% alcohol can be placed in the tin. Many different types of bait, for example rotten meat or fermenting fruit, can be put in the tin next to the bottle of alcohol. A roof to protect the trap from rain can be made by balancing a plate on three stones, with a large stone on top to prevent it blowing away. Holes and ditches with steep sides, such as water furrows, often make good natural pitfalls.

Collecting in grass and shrubs

To collect in grass and shrubs, walk through a field sweeping a net from side to side through the grass, constantly flipping it over to keep the open end facing forward. After a while, fold the end of the net over the frame. When you want to empty the net, have an aspirator and killing bottle at the ready. (Beware: angry wasps are usually the first to fly out!) A large variety of insects will be found at the bottom of the net, along with bits of grass and seeds. The sweep net can also be held out of the window of a slow-moving vehicle.

Collecting in trees and shrubs

When one approaches trees and shrubs, the insects seem either to fly away, fall to the ground or hide behind branches. However, with some patience and experience, they can often be caught using a killing bottle and its lid. Insects can also be beaten out of trees or shrubs on to a sheet of cloth stretched over a wooden cross. This apparatus is held under a suitable branch, which is then rapped hard with a stout stick. Remember to have the aspirator ready to catch jumping and flying insects.

Larvae found on the branches can be bred to the adult stage simply by tying a chiffon bag around them on a branch of their host plant, together with an ample supply of fresh leaves. If the larva pupates in soil, a handful of soil must also be placed in the chiffon bag. Protect against ants by smearing poison or ant glue around the base of the branches. Insects in galls and seeds can be bred out in bottles at home. Remember to cover the opening of the bottle with gauze for ventilation. Dead and decaying wood also form the home of many insects. The bark of dead trees can be broken off and the wood split to discover the insects.

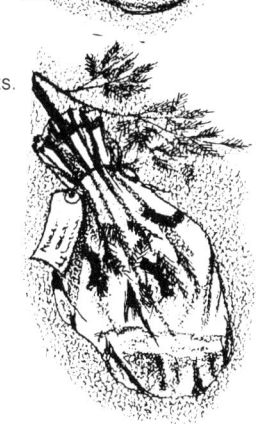

Collecting flying insects

Besides the ordinary net, you can also make use of traps to collect day-flying insects. Yellow or blue dishes containing a little soapy water will attract and then drown the insects.

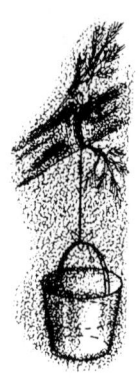

Fruit beetles can easily be collected in a bucket of fermenting fruit bait, hung high in a tree. Ensure that the walls of the bucket are smooth and that its depth is greater than its diameter.

At night, flying insects can be attracted to a light. The brighter the light and the more ultra-violet it contains, the better. Hang the light in front of a white sheet, which should extend on to the floor to catch the falling insects. You will collect many insects in the early part of the evening but the less common insects often make their appearance later on. On windy or bright, moonlit nights, you will have very little success with light traps.

Collecting water insects

A variety of interesting insects can be collected by drawing a net through a pond or open reservoir. You can also make an underwater light trap by lowering a waterproof torch attached to a string into the water. In front of the torch make a cylinder of mosquito-wire gauze which, at its furthest point, is bent back to form a funnel with an entry hole of approximately 12 mm. Insects swim towards the light, into the funnel and then cannot find their way out.

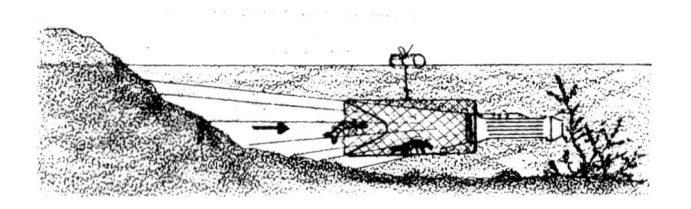

How to preserve your insect collection

If the insects are not mounted correctly and properly looked after, your collection may be eaten by insect pests, thrown away in error, or go to waste in one way or the other.

Preparation for mounting

Insects which have been freshly killed or have been kept in alcohol or ethyl acetate can be mounted directly on pins. Insects which have dried out can be softened by leaving them in a sealed plastic container together with damp tissue paper. A few drops of formaldehyde will prevent fungi from forming.

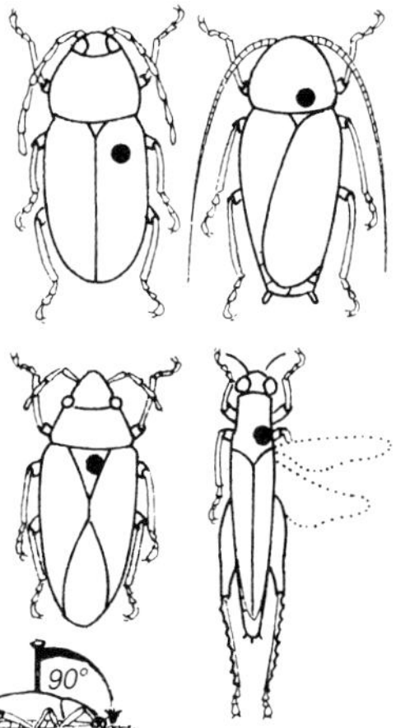

Pinning of insects

Insects with a length exceeding 8 mm are usually mounted directly on pins. Insect pins are longer than normal pins, will not rust and are available in different diameters. A pin should be thick enough to hold and support an insect firmly in place, but not so thick that it damages the specimen. In addition to pins, you will need a setting board, grooved setting boards, a mounting step, smooth paper and a sturdy pair of tweezers.

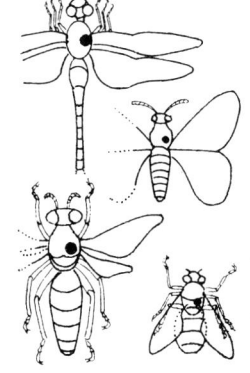

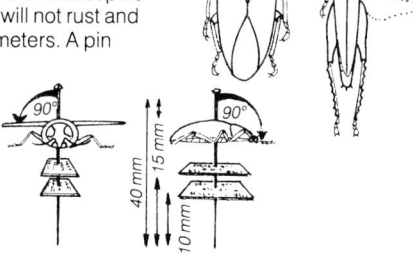

Insert the pins through the specimen in the position marked on the sketches, according to the specific insect group. Make sure that the pin is at a 90° angle in both directions.

The mounting step is used to ensure that all insects are mounted at a uniform height on the pins. When the insects are mounted and dry, the step is used to ensure that all labels are on the same level.

Make a setting board from a block of polystyrene about 300 mm square and cover it with a piece of thin paper. Push a pin through the insect into the setting board until the underside of the insect touches the papered surface.

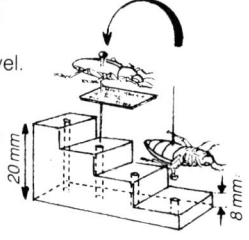

Arrange the feelers and legs in a natural position and hold them in place with temporary pins. Leave the insect to dry for approximately a week.

Insects whose wings must be set in the open position (for example, butterflies and dragonflies) are mounted on a grooved setting board (soft wood is the most suitable material to use). The groove must be as wide as the insect's body. Thin paper or cellophane strips are used to hold open the wings. Do not insert pins through the wings. The wings must be mounted in such a way that the rear margin of the forewing is at 90° to the body. Support the abdomen in the groove with a few pins or a folded strip of paper. Allow to dry for about a week.

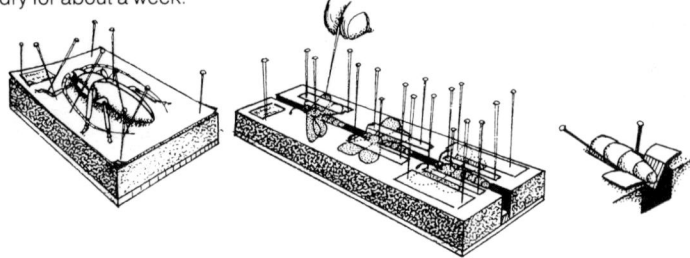

Mounting on minuten pins

Small insects (3-8 mm) are mounted on minuten pins, which are very thin insect pins (usually without heads). Mount a thin strip of cork or polyporus on to a normal insect pin, then stick the minuten pins into it. The minuten pins are best handled with tweezers. They can be inserted into the insect's body either from above or below. The labels are placed on the normal pin.

Mounting on cardboard platforms

Very small insects (0,5-3 mm) or those which are too thin to be pinned, are stuck on to cardboard platforms, 5 x 10 mm. First mount the cardboard on to a normal pin, then put a small drop of paper glue on the cardboard. The insect is picked up with a wet pin or thin paintbrush and carefully manoeuvred on to the drop of glue. Do not put too much glue on the cardboard, otherwise it will show under the insect's body, or worse, be smeared all over it. Spread out the legs and feelers with a pin.

In the case of ants, where there are different castes (for example, workers, soldiers and queen)

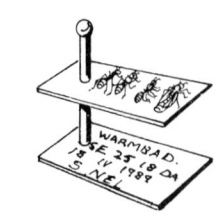

within the species, simply stick them alongside one another on a platform.

Small gnats, flies, mosquitoes and wasps are best mounted by cutting the platform to a sharp point, bending the tip slightly, and sticking the side of the insect's thorax against this point.

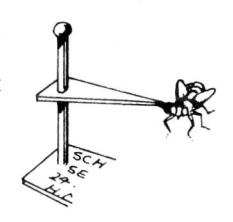

Labels

To be of any value, every insect mounted must have a label displaying the following information: locality where collected, giving the degrees and minutes of latitude and longitude; the date when collected; and the name of the collector. Labels should be approximately 10 x 20 mm in size. Any information regarding habitat, behaviour and collecting methods which could be of importance can be noted on a second label which is pinned beneath the main label.

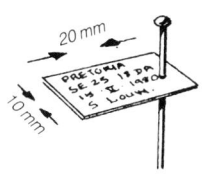

Mounting in capsules

Empty medical gelatine capsules are ideal for preserving very small insects such as fleas, lice, booklice, parasitic wasps and aphids. One half of the capsule is pinned, the insect is placed in the other half and secured with a wad of cottonwool. The half of the capsule containing the insect is then positioned on the pinned half. Capsules can also be used to protect insects on platforms from being damaged.

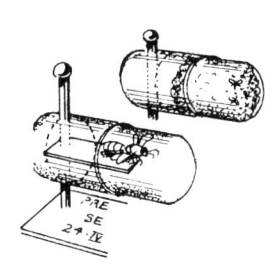

Preserving in alcohol

Larvae, caterpillars, termites and other soft insect samples must be kept in alcohol to prevent them drying out and shrivelling. Find a pill bottle with a tight seal and, using cottonwool, hold the insect specimen in position against the inside of the bottle. Fill the bottle with 70-80% alcohol. For the following three days, replace the alcohol each day. The label (written in Indian ink or pencil) must be put into the bottle and be visible next to the insect.

An alcohol collection must either be kept in the refrigerator or the bottles refilled regularly.

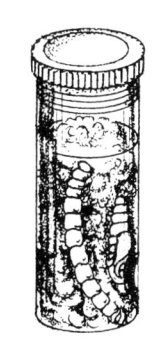

Preservation of the collection

Insects which have been pinned and dried will keep for hundreds of years without any preserving agent. They are, however, very brittle and must therefore be well protected. They will be eaten by other insects if these are not kept at bay.
The collection should thus be kept in a drawer or box with a sealed lid, and insect repellent used. A cardboard box-file can be used to make an insect box: stick a layer of thin, paper-covered cork on the bottom, cut out the lid and stick a thin glass pane on the inside.

Large collections are best preserved in wooden drawers with glass lids. These drawers usually contain movable cardboard boxes, bottom-lined with cork or polystyrene.

Mothballs or plastic strips with dichlorvos (commercially available as 'Vapona' strips) can be put in the drawer or container as protection against insects. These should be replaced three times a year.

Glossary

abdomen — hind body of an insect.
antenna/*pl.* -e — feelers on the 'forehead' of an insect.
aquatic — living in water.
backplate — the part of an insect's skin or shell that covers the upper side of each segment.
calcrete — sedementary rock formation.
cerc/us, *pl.* -i — pair of 'tails' or appendages on the rear end of an insect.
compound eyes — the normal eyes of adult insects, consisting of many facets.
coxa, *pl.* -e — the 'hip joint' of an insect leg, connecting the leg to the body.
cremaster — the tip of the tail of a butterfly pupa, which is covered with fine hooks.
dun — the stage in a mayfly's development, after the nymph and before the adult.
elytr/on, *pl.* -a — hardened forewings in beetles.
fem/ur, *pl.* -ora — 'thigh' or upper part of leg in insects.
halteres — reduced hind wings in flies.
herbivores — plant feeders.
hopper — an immature locust.
instar — life stage between moults, e.g. second larval instar is the larva after hatching and moulting once.
lamellate — made up of flat layers, like a booklet.
maggot — legless larva of a fly.
mandibles — set of biting mouthparts of insects.
ocell/us, *pl.* -i — simple (not compound) eyes on the 'forehead' of insects.
ovipositor — egg-laying tube or apparatus in female insects.
petiole — thin segments between thorax and abdomen in ants, bees and wasps (actually part of abdomen).
proboscis — tube-like, elongated mouthparts of insects.
pronotum — back-plate of first segment of thorax, in most insects covering the whole thorax.
ringbark — to cut the bark around a tree or branch, killing off the limb above the cut.
rostrum — snout or elongated head, with mouthparts at the tip.
segment — a distinct plate or part of an insect's skin or armour.
tars/us, *pl.* -i — 'foot' or last part of an insect leg, usually consisting of several small segments.
thorax — 'breast-plate' or part of the insect body between head and abdomen.
tibia, *pl.* -e — 'shin' or lower part of leg of insects.

Further reading

General identification
Scholtz, C.H. and Holm, E. (eds.) 1985. *Insects of Southern Africa*. Butterworths, Durban.

Pest insects
Annecke, D.P. and Moran, V.C. 1982. *Insects and Mites of Cultivated Plants in South Africa*. Butterworths, Pretoria.

Biology and methods
Brits, J.A. 1984. *Chemical Defence in Insects*. Insight Series. De Jager-HAUM, Pretoria.
De Villiers, W.M. 1982. *Grasshoppers and Locusts*. Insight Series. De Jager-HAUM, Pretoria.
Holm, E. 1982. *Ants*. Insight Series. De Jager-HAUM, Pretoria.
Londt, J.G.H. 1984. *A Beginner's Guide to Insects*. Wildlife Society of Southern Africa.
Schoeman, A.S. 1985. *Praying Mantids and Stick Insects*. Insight Series. De Jager-HAUM, Pretoria.
Scholtz, C.H. 1984. *Useful Insects*. Insight Series. De Jager-HAUM, Pretoria.
Scholtz, C.H. and de Villiers, W.M. 1983. *Dung Beetles*. Insight Series. De Jager-HAUM, Pretoria.
Skaife, S.H. 1979 (revised edition). *African Insect Life*. C. Struik, Cape Town.
Smithers, C. 1982. *Handbook of Insect Collecting*. Delta Books, Johannesburg.

(Several other titles are in preparation for the Insight Series.)

INDEX

Numbers in **bold type** indicate the main subject entry.

A
Acraeidae 40
Alderflies 8, **49**
ametabolic life cycle 51
Anisoptera 10
Anthophoridae 48
Antlions 7, 8, **24**
Ants 44, **48**
   Velvet **45**
Aphidoidea 23
Aphids **23**
Apidae 47
Arthropoda 5
Asilidae 38

B
Back-swimmers 20
Bees 8, 44, **47**
   Carpenter **48**
   Honey **47**
   Leafcutter **47**
   Mocca **47**
   Mopane **47**
   Solitary **47**
Beetles 7, **25**
   Ant **25**
   Blister **30**
   'brush' **29**
   Click **29**
   CMR **30**
   Darkling **32**
   Dung **28**
   Flat **30**
   Flower **30**
   'goliath' **28**
   Ground **26**
   Harlequin **27**
   Jewel **29**
   Leaf **34**
   Leaf-mining **34**
   Rhinoceros **27**
   Rove **27**
   Snouted **35**
   Spotted maize **30**
   Stag **27**
   Tenebrionid **32**
   Tiger **25**
   Tortoise **34**
   Water **26**
Belastomatidae 20
Besies 17
   Grys- **19**
   Lantern- **22**
   Skildstink- **20**
   Skuim- **22**
   Son- **21**
   Verwelk- **19**
   Vlek- **18**
Blaaspootjies 50
Bladspringers 22

Blattodea 7, **9**, 51
Bloutjies 39
Blues **39**
Boktorre 33
Bombyliidae 38
Booklice 8, **49**
Boomspringers 22
Borers, Flat-headed 29
   Lily 35
   Shot-hole **31**
   Stem 42
Bostrychidae 31
Brachycera 37, 38
Bugs 8, **17**
   Assassin **18**
   Bed **18**
   Lantern **22**
   Mealy **23**
   Seed **19**
   Shield **20**
   Spittle **22**
   Water **20**
Buprestidae 29
Butterflies 8, **39**
   Nymphalid **40**
Bye 47
   Alleenloper- 47
   Blaarsnyer- 47
   Houtkapper- 48
   Perde- 46

C
Caddisflies 7, 8, **50**
Caelifera 15
Calliphoridae 37
Carabidae 26
Cassidinae 34
Centipedes 5
Cerambycidae 33
Cercopidae 22
Cetoniinae 28
Chalcidoidea 44
Charaxidae 40
Chrysididae 45
Chrysomelidae 34
Chrysopidae 24
Cicadas **21**
Cicadelloidea 22
Cicadidae 21
Cicindelidae 25
Cimicidae 18
Coccidae 23
Coccinellidae 31
Cockroaches 7, **9**
Coleoptera 7, 25-35, 52
Coppers **39**
Coreidae 19
Crickets 7, **14**
   Mole 14
Culicidae 36
Curculionidae 35
Cyclorrhapha 36, 37, 38

D
Damselflies 6, **10**
Danaidae 39
Dermaptera 7, 11, 51
Diaspididae 23
Diopsidae 36
Diptera 8, 36, 37, 38, 52
Dragonflies 6, **10**
Dubbelsterte 40
Dynastinae 27
Dytiscidae 26

E
Earwigs 7, 11
Eendagvlieë 10
Elateridae 29
Embiidina 7, 49, 51
Ensifera 14
Ephemeroptera 6, 10, 52
Eumenidae 46
Eumolpinae 34
Eupterotidae 43

F
Fireflies 30
Fishmoths 6, **9**, 51
Fleas 6, **50**
Flies 8, **36**
   Bee **38**
   Blow **37**
   Crane **36**
   Fruit **37**
   Horse **37**
   Louse **38**
   Red-headed **38**
   Robber **38**
   Stalk-eyed **36**
'fool's gold' beetles 34
Formicidae 48
Fruit chafers **28**
Fulgoroidea 22

G
Geometridae 44
Gerridae 20
Goudogies 24
Grasshoppers **15**
   Crested 16
   Milkweed 16
   Toad 16
Gryllidae 14
Gryllotalpidae 14
Gyrinidae 26

H
Halictidae 47
Hanging flies 6, **50**
hemimetabolic life cycle 51, 52
Hemiptera 8, 17-23, 51
Heteroptera 17, 18, 19, 20, 21
Hippoboscidae 38
Hispinae 34
Histeridae 27
holometabolic life cycle 52
Homoptera 17, 21, 22, 23

Hottentotsgotte 13
   Vals- 24
Hymenoptera 8, 44-48, 52

I
Ichneumonoidea 44
Isoptera 7, 12, 51

K
Kakkerlakke 9
Katydids **14**
Kewers 25
   Blaarmyn- 34
   Blaartrek- 30
   Blaarvlerk- 30
   Blaarvreet- 34
   Blom- 30
   CMR- 30
   Grootkaak- 27
   Harlekyn- 27
   Klatergoud- 34
   Kortskild- 27
   Mier- 25
   Prag- 29
   Renoster- 27
   Skilpad- 31
   Snuit- 35
   Tier- 25
   Water- 26
Kniptorre 29
Kopertjies 39
Krieke 14
   Mol- 14

L
Lacewings 7, 8, **24**
   Ribbon-winged **24**
Ladybirds **31**
Lampyridae 30
Landmeters 44
Langasempies 14
Leafhoppers **22**
Lepelvlerkies 24
Lepidoptera 8, 39-44, 52
Lice 8, **17**
Locusts 7, **15**
Longicorns **33**
Loopers **44**
Lucanidae 27
Luise 17
   Boek- 49
   Dop- 23
   Plant- 23
   Wee- 18
   Wol- 23
Lycaenidae 39
Lycidae 30
Lygaeidae 19

M
Mantidfly **24**
Mantids, praying 7, **13**
Mantispidae 24
Mantodea 7, 13, 51
Mayflies 6, **10**

Mecoptera 6, 50, 52
Megachilidae 47
Megaloptera 7, 8, 49, 52
Meloidae 30
Melyridae 30
Membracidae 22
metamorphosis 51, 52
Miere 48
   Fluweel- 45
Mierleeus 24
Millipedes 5
Miskruiers 28
Mites 5
Monarchs **39**
Mosquitoes 8, **36**
Moths 8, **39**
   Day-flying **43**
   Emperor **41**
   Hawk **42**
   Owl **42**
Motte 39
   Dagvlieënde 43
   Pou-oog- 41
   Pylstert- 42
   Uil- 42
   Water- 50
Muscidae 37
Muskiete 36
   Langbeen- 36
Mutillidae 45
Myrmeleontidae 24

N
Naaldekokers 11
Nematocera 36
Nemopteridae 24
Nepidae 21
Neuroptera 7, 8, 24, 52
Noctuidae 42
Notonectidae 20
Nymphalidae 40

O
Odonata 6, 10, 52
Oogskieters 26
Oorkruipers 11
Orthoptera 7, 14, 15, 51

P
Papilionidae 40
Paussidae 25
Pentatomoidea 20
Phasmatodea 7, 17, 51
Phthiraptera 8, 17, 51
Pieridae 39
Platystomatidae 38
Plecoptera 7, 49, 52
Pompilidae 45
Pond skaters **20**
Pseudococcidae 23
Psocoptera 8, 49, 51
Psychidae 43
Pyrrhocoridae 18

R
Reds **40**
Reduviidae 18
Roofwantse 18
Rooitjies **40**
Rugswemmers 20

S
Sakwurms 43
Saturniidae 41
Scale insects **23**
Scarabaeidae 27, 28
Scarabaeinae 28
Scorpions 5
   Water 21
Silverfish **9**
Silwervisse 9
Siphonaptera 6, 50, 52
Skaapbrommers 37
Skoenlappers 39
   Borselpoot- 40
   Melkbos- 39
Sphecidae 46
Sphingidae 42
Spiders 5
Spinnekopjagters 45
Sprinkane 15
   Trek- 15
Stainers **18**
   Cotton 18
Staphylinidae 27
Stick insects 7, **17**
Stokinsekte 17
Stompkopboorders 31
Stoneflies 7, **49**
Swaelsterte 40
Swallowtails **40**
Swifts **40**

T
Tabanidae 37
Tenebrionidae 32
Tephritidae 37
Termiete 12
Termites 7, **12**
Thrips 7, **50**
Thysanoptera 7, 50, 51
Thysanura 6, 9, 51
Ticks 5
Tipulidae 36
Toktokkies 32
Tonnelspinners 49
Treehoppers **22**
Trichoptera 7, 8, 50, 52
Tweevlerkiges 36
Twig wilters **19**

V
Vespidae 46
Vismotte 9
Vlieë 37
   Blinde- 37
   By- 38
   Hang- 50
   Kameelnek- 49
   Luis- 38
   Pêrel- 49
   Roof- 38
   Rooikop- 38
   Steeloog- 36
   Vrugte- 37
Vliesvlerke 44
Vlooie 50
Vrugtetorre 28
Vuurvliegies 30

W
Wasps 8, **44**
   Cuckoo **45**
   Digger **46**
   Mud **46**
   Paper **46**
   Parasitic **44**
   Potter **46**
   Spider **45**
Waterhondjies 26
Waterjuffers 10
Waterlopers 20
Waterskerpioene 21
Waterwantse, reuse 20
Web spinners 7, **49**
Weevils **35**
   Cycad **35**
   Granary 35
   Leaf-rolling 35
Wespes
   Graaf- 46
   Klei- 46
   Koekoek- 45
   Parasiet- 44
   Pottebakker- 46
Whirligigs **26**
Whites **39**
Witjies 39
Wolhaarruspes 43
Woolly bears **43**
Worms
   Bag **43**
   Boll 42
   Commando 42
   Cut 42
   Glow 30
   Mopane 41
   Wire 29

X
Xylocopinae 48

Z
Zygaenidae 43
Zygoptera 10